NEW
EVERY
MORNING

NEW EDITION
1973

NEW EVERY MORNING

(NEW EDITION)

A BOOK OF DAILY SERVICES
FOR BROADCASTING

New every morning is the love
Our wakening and uprising prove;
Through sleep and darkness safely brought,
Restored to life, and power, and thought.

JOHN KEBLE

LONDON
THE BRITISH BROADCASTING
CORPORATION
1983

Published by the British Broadcasting Corporation
35 Marylebone High Street, London WIM 4AA

ISBN: 0 563 12193 9 (cloth)
ISBN: 0 563 12243 9 (paper)

First published 1973
Reprinted 1974, 1976, 1977, 1979, 1982, 1983

© British Broadcasting Corporation 1973

Printed in Great Britain at the
University Press, Cambridge

CONTENTS

THE DAILY SERVICE

GOD THE THREE IN ONE

THE PATTERN PRAYER

ACKNOWLEDGEMENTS

The texts of the Authorised Version of the Bible and the 1662 Book of Common Prayer are Crown Copyright and the extracts from them used herein are reproduced by permission. Extracts from the Prayer Book as proposed in 1928 are printed with the permission of the Holder of the Copyright. Extracts from Alternative Services Series 3, An Order for Holy Communion, are reprinted by permission of SPCK on behalf of the Registrars of the Provinces of Canterbury and York, and of the International Consultation on English Texts.

Thanks are due to the following for permission to reprint or adapt for broadcasting other prayers used in this book:

Edward Arnold (Publishers) Ltd (*Words for Worship* by C. R. Campling and M. Davis); Church Missionary Society (*Prayer Card*; *Put Prayer First*); Church Pastoral-Aid Society (*Family Worship*; *Prayers for Today's Church*); James Clarke & Co. Ltd (*The Norton Prayer Book* by J. Wilson; *The Book of Common Worship* by James Ferguson); Coventry Cathedral; Darton, Longman and Todd Ltd (*Catholic Prayer Book*); Epworth Press (*The Methodist Church Book of Offices*); Hodder and Stoughton Ltd (*Parish Prayers* by Frank Colquhoun); Mayhew-McCrimmon Ltd (*The One Who Listens* by Michael Hollings and Etta Gullick); Mowbrays (*The Prayer Manual*); Oxford University Press (*Daily Prayer*, compiled by Eric Milner-White and G. W. Briggs; *A Diocesan Service Book*, edited and ordered by Bishop Leslie Stannard Hunter, adapted by permission; *The Book of Common Order* and *Prayers for the Christian Year*, both by permission of the Committee on Public Worship and Aids to Devotion of the Church of Scotland); Saint Andrew Press (*Prayers for Use in Church* by J. W. G. Masterton; *Together in Worship*); Scripture Union (*Prayers*); Society for Promoting Christian Knowledge (*The Broadcast Psalter*; *The Splendour of God*; *Prayer and the Departed* by Ian Ramsey; *The Daily Office*, by permission of the Joint Liturgical Group; *Calendars and Lessons*, with acknowledgement to the Rev. K. T. Street and the Liturgical Commission of the Church of England); SCM Press Ltd (*A Book of Prayers for Schools*; *Contemporary Prayers for Public Worship*, edited by Caryl Micklem; *Epilogue and Prayers* by William Barclay); The United Society for the Propagation of the Gospel ('Prayer is my Life' by Margaret Dewey); the Most Rev. George Appleton; the Rev. Llewellyn Cumings; the Ven. T. Dudley-Smith; Mrs M. E. Forrester (for a prayer by the Rev. C. R. Forrester); Miss Phoebe Hesketh; the Rev. Caryl Micklem; Canon C. B. Naylor; the Rt Rev. R. A. Reeves; Mrs Anne Ridler; the Rev. J. R. W. Stott; the Rev. J. M. Todd; the Rev. R. Tomes.

FOREWORD

By His Grace the Lord Archbishop of Canterbury

New Every Morning enters upon a further period of its life in a form which is recognisably the same and yet adapted in the light of the experience of praying and worshipping Christians in the last few years. The changes chiefly to be noticed are in the range of the subjects for prayer in our sad and bewildered world and in the kind of language which is used.

Is prayer in contemporary English a good thing? If the language is self-consciously modern and full of jargon and cliché, No. But if the language is simple and natural, Yes. The old language of the Prayer Book which many have loved for centuries was once new and contemporary, and we need not be afraid of change. Our Heavenly Father, we are sure, wishes us to speak to him in a natural, everyday way. Many of the prayers in this new edition express this.

The book will, however, be seen to retain much that is old while also including much that is new. Many loved phrases from the past will be found. True prayer will always speak from the heart of our contemporary world and at the same time recollect the timeless, unchanging character of God in his mystery, greatness and goodness.

MICHAEL CANTUAR:

The Old Palace
Canterbury
January 1973

INTRODUCTION

THIS latest edition of *New Every Morning* is an attempt to bring the book – and therefore the broadcast Daily Service – more into line with current needs. In general the prayers have been phrased in contemporary language instead of in the traditional 'thee, thou' idiom; and the opportunity has been taken of introducing a certain amount of new material. Over one hundred and fifty prayers have been written for the book and here make their first appearance in print. They cover a wider variety of subjects and intentions than the earlier editions provided and relate more directly to some at least of the major issues that confront us all in the late twentieth century: contrasting affluence and poverty, for instance, the advance of science and technology, the use and abuse of natural resources, race relations, the confrontation with unbelief and the 'crisis of faith'.

At the same time it must be made clear that this is not an entirely new book. Much of the old material, suitably revised and adapted, has been retained. Certain ancient prayers and collects have been left unaltered; and at least one of these has been included in each service. The familiar daily themes have been conserved under new titles, along with the basic structure of the services. This means that each section opens, as before, with a sung sentence or introit (some new ones have now been introduced), leading into an act of worship based on the theme for the day. After the psalm or canticle and the Scripture reading there follow groups of prayers of petition and intercession, which develop the theme; and the service ends each time with a hymn and a blessing. The prayers in the main body of the book are supplemented by a section at the end entitled 'Intercessions for a Week', together with some prayers for occasional use. The collects for Holy Days from the Book of Common Prayer are also included, as in the two previous editions.

The work of revision has been carried out by Canon Frank Colquhoun, formerly of Southwark, now of Norwich Cathedral; and we wish to express our gratitude and thanks to him for the help he has given. In addition to acting as compiler and co-editor he has written a considerable number of the new prayers. Others who have contributed fresh material at our invitation are Canon Basil Naylor, the Rev. James M. Todd, the Rev. Roger Tomes, the Ven. Timothy Dudley-Smith, the Rev. Caryl Micklem, the Rev. John Stott, and Miss Phoebe Hesketh. We acknowledge our indebtedness to them all.

The task now completed marks a further stage in the story of *New Every Morning* and the Daily Service. When the Daily Service was first broadcast in 1928, a small collection of the prayers used was put together by the Rev. Hugh Johnston and was published under the title *This Day*. This was followed in 1932 by *When Two or Three*, which was an expanded version of *This Day* but with the prayers grouped round a general theme and with the addition of suitable psalms and hymns.

In 1936 the first edition of *New Every Morning* appeared, edited by the Rev. Dr F. A. Iremonger, at that time the BBC's Director of Religion, who was assisted by a committee. When war broke out in 1939, a large number of new prayers came into use in the Daily Service, in order to meet the special needs of the time; and Dr Iremonger, who had by then become Dean of Lichfield, prepared a book of services suitable for wartime use, entitled *Each Returning Day*. After the war a new edition of *New Every Morning* was called for and was put together by the Rev.

Eric Fenn in consultation with the staff of the Religious Broadcasting Department. Published in 1948, this was a major revision, bringing together all that was appropriate in the previous edition and the additional material which had been accumulated during and after the war. With this revision the service acquired its present form. A revision in 1955 made only minor alterations, but included for the first time the collects for Holy Days. The most recent revision was carried out in 1961 under the supervision of the Rev. J. A. Fisher, Canon of Windsor, who had been on the staff of the Religious Broadcasting Department.

The continued demand for *New Every Morning* since it first appeared in 1936 encourages us to believe that it meets a genuine need, providing as it does a handbook for those who regularly listen to the Daily Service and a devotional aid for others who find in its pages something to help them in their own private prayers. We hope that this new edition will fulfil the same dual purpose at least as competently as its predecessors.

HUBERT HOSKINS

Our Father, who art in heaven,
hallowed be thy name;
thy kingdom come;
thy will be done;
on earth as it is in heaven.
Give us this day our daily bread.
And forgive us our trespasses,
as we forgive those who trespass against us.
And lead us not into temptation;
but deliver us from evil.
For thine is the Kingdom, the power
and the glory, for ever and ever.   Amen.

Or this:

Our Father in heaven,
hallowed be your Name,
your kingdom come,
your will be done,
on earth as in heaven.
Give us today our daily bread.
Forgive us our sins
as we forgive those who sin against us.
Do not bring us to the time of trial
but deliver us from evil.

For the kingdom, the power, and the glory are yours
now and for ever.   Amen.

HOLY IS THE LORD

Holy, holy, holy, Lord God of hosts; heaven and earth are full of thy glory. Glory be to thee, O Lord most high.

O worship the Lord in the beauty of holiness; let the whole earth stand in awe of him.

ALMIGHTY God, to whom all hearts are open,
all desires known,
and from whom no secrets are hid:
cleanse the thoughts of our hearts
by the inspiration of your Holy Spirit,
that we may perfectly love you,
and worthily magnify your holy name;
through Christ our Lord.

HYMN

GOD is spirit: and those who worship him must worship
in spirit and in truth.

God is light: if we walk in the light, as he is in the light, we have fellowship with one another.

God is love: everyone who loves is born of God and knows God; and we know that we have passed out of death into life because we love the brethren.

Father, Lord of heaven and earth, we confess to you all the hidden and open sins of our hearts and minds; and we ask of you, the merciful and righteous judge, forgiveness for the past and grace to sin no more; through Jesus Christ our Lord.

OUR FATHER...

CANTICLE OR PSALM

BIBLE READING

O GOD, our Judge and Saviour, set before us the vision of your purity, and let us see our sins in the light of your holiness. Pierce our self-contentment with the shafts of your burning love, and let that love consume in us all that hinders us from perfect service of your cause; for as your holiness is our judgement, so are your wounds our salvation.

Holy God, in whose kingdom there is nothing that works evil or makes a lie: help us by your grace to guard our words, to keep our promises, and to speak the truth; for the honour of our Lord Jesus Christ.

A collect

ALMIGHTY and everlasting God, who art always more ready to hear than we to pray, and art wont to give more than either we desire or deserve: pour down upon us the abundance of thy mercy; forgiving us those things whereof our conscience is afraid, and giving us those good things which we are not worthy to ask, but through the merits and mediation of Jesus Christ, thy Son, our Lord.

FAITH IN GOD

ETERNAL God, whose kingdom is from everlasting to everlasting: speak to our hearts when courage fails and love grows cold and there is distress of nations on the earth. Keep us resolute and steadfast in the things that cannot be shaken; restore our faith in your eternal purpose; and renew in us the hope that never fails; through Jesus Christ our Lord.

O God our Father, by whom we are called
    to ventures of which we cannot see the ending
    and by paths as yet untrodden:
give us faith to go out always with good courage,
    knowing that in your power alone we are made strong
and that your love will never fail us,
    in Jesus Christ our Lord.

O God of infinite love and power, give us grace to
believe that the things which are impossible with men are
possible with you. Save us from all doubt of your goodness
and questioning of your love; and help us so to trust in
your wisdom and mercy that we may be calm and unafraid.

THOSE WHO DOUBT

O GOD, whose Son our Lord Jesus Christ has promised
that those who follow him shall not walk in darkness
but shall have the light of life: have mercy on all who are
afflicted by doubt or perplexity amid the mysteries of life;
and enable them so to see the light of Christ that they may
learn to walk humbly by faith in him and find rest for their
souls.

Most merciful God, we pray
    for those who doubt your love;
    for those who find it difficult to believe or to pray;
    for those who have lost a faith they once possessed.
May the Holy Spirit enlighten their minds
    and lead them into all truth,
through Jesus Christ our Lord.

JUDGES AND MAGISTRATES

O GOD, the Judge of all men, give to those who minister justice the spirit of wisdom and discernment; and that they may be strong and patient, upright and compassionate, fill them, O Lord, with the spirit of your holy fear.

FOR THE DAY

ETERNAL God and Father, by whose power we are created and by whose love we are redeemed: guide and strengthen us by your Spirit, that we may give ourselves to your service, and live this day in love to one another and to you; through Jesus Christ our Lord.

Almighty God bless us with his Holy Spirit this day;
    guard us in our going out and coming in;
keep us ever steadfast in our faith,
    free from sin and safe from danger;
through Jesus Christ our Lord.

HYMN

THE BLESSING

GLORY BE TO GOD ON HIGH

O magnify the Lord with me, and let us exalt his name together.

O praise God in his holiness; praise him in the firmament of his power.

OPEN our eyes, O God, to your glory, that we may worship in spirit and in truth, and offer you the praise of glad and thankful hearts.

HYMN

GLORY be to God, Maker of heaven and earth,
for calling the worlds into being
    and bringing order and beauty out of chaos;
    for awakening man to desire him
    and to thirst after truth.
Glory be to God for his mighty acts in the redemption of mankind:
    for sending forth his Son in the fullness of time
    to be born,
    to live and work,
    to seek and save the lost,
    to suffer and die,
    and to rise victorious over death.
Glory be to God for his Holy Spirit, ever working in the hearts of men,
    to lead us into truth
    and point the way to goodness,
    by whose grace we are enabled now to pray
    as our Saviour Christ taught us:

OUR FATHER...

CANTICLE OR PSALM

BIBLE READING

GRANT us, O God, to see in all the beauty of the world around us the reflection of your own eternal glory. Open our eyes to all the signs of your love, and enable us so to live that we may hold all created things in reverence for your sake who made them; through Jesus Christ our Lord.

Heavenly Father, who revealed your glory in the face of Jesus Christ: help us so to live in him and he in us that our lives may reflect his beauty and magnify his name.

A collect

O GOD, who declarest thy almighty power most chiefly in showing mercy and pity: mercifully grant unto us such a measure of thy grace, that we, running the way of thy commandments, may obtain thy gracious promises, and be made partakers of thy heavenly treasure; through Jesus Christ our Lord.

SOCIAL ORDER

O GOD our Father, increase among us, and in every nation, the sense of human brotherhood, true respect for man and for woman, loyalty in service, happiness in work, and a just reward for labour; that our homes may be kept safe and pure, our cities renewed in beauty and order, and all the world reflect the radiance of your kingdom; through Jesus Christ our Lord.

Almighty Father, whose love enfolds all your children: we confess with shame and penitence the disorder, injustice and misery which are among us; and we pray that, looking to you for pardon and grace, we may henceforth set ourselves to establish that city which has justice for its foundation and love for its law; through Jesus Christ our Lord.

Almighty God, who created man in your own image and for the service of your kingdom: give us grace fearlessly to contend against evil and to make no peace with oppression; and that we may reverently use our freedom, help us to employ it for the increase of justice among men and nations, to the glory of your holy name.

INTERNATIONAL JUSTICE AND ORDER

OVERRULE, O God, the passions and designs of men. Let your strong hand control the nations and bring forth, out of present discord, a harmony more perfect than we can conceive; a new humility, a new understanding, a new hunger and thirst for righteousness; that your will may be done on earth as it is in heaven.

God of the nations, whose kingdom rules over all,
    have mercy on our broken and divided world.
Shed abroad your peace in the hearts of men
    and banish from them the spirit that makes for war;
that all races and peoples may learn to live
    as members of one family
    and in obedience to your laws;
through Jesus Christ our Lord.

We pray, O God, for the leaders of the nations; that building on the foundations of justice, truth and freedom, they may unite men everywhere in the bonds of peace, for the glory of your name.

FOR THE DAY

INTO your hands, O merciful God, we commit ourselves and those we love. Give to each one of us a watchful, humble and diligent spirit, that we may seek in all things to know and to do your will, to the honour of Christ our Lord.

> Lord God, whose we are and whom we serve,
> help us to glorify you this day
>> in all the thoughts of our hearts,
>> in all the words of our lips,
>> and in all the works of our hands,
> as becomes those who are your servants,
> through Jesus Christ our Lord.

HYMN

THE BLESSING

3

MAKER OF ALL THINGS

All thy works praise thee, O Lord; and thy saints give thanks unto thee.

O come, let us worship and fall down; let us kneel before the Lord our maker.

O Lord, thou hast searched me out and known me; whither shall I go then from thy presence?

O GOD, most holy, most loving, infinite in wisdom and power: teach us to reverence you in all the works of your hands, and to hallow your name both in our lives and in our worship; through Jesus Christ our Lord.

HYMN

GOD our Father, Creator and Lord of all things, the earth belongs to you. Land and sea and air, all are yours, and so are the vast galaxies of space. Nothing is beyond your power, nothing is beneath your notice.

For you are a loving Father to your great family. You provide for our needs, you steady us when we stumble, you help us when we fall. May we always give thanks to you, in the way we live as well as in the things we say.

We are ashamed that we have done so badly in the past, forgetting your kingdom and serving our own pleasure. Father, forgive us and renew us; let your light and truth lead us; through Jesus Christ our Lord.

OUR FATHER...

CANTICLE OR PSALM

BIBLE READING

Awaken us, O God, to your presence, that we may walk in your world as your children. Give us reverence for all creation, that we may treat all living things with gentleness and our fellow men with courtesy; through Jesus Christ our Lord.

Show us, O God, how to love not only animals, birds, and all green and growing things, but the soil, air and water by which we live, so that we may not exploit and pollute them for our own profit or convenience. Help us to cherish these necessities for our survival; and guide those in authority to ensure that the human spirit may not be starved in pursuit of material comfort and wealth.

Lord of the universe, we praise you for your creation: for the wonder of space, the beauty of the world, and the value of earth's resources. Keep us from spoiling these gifts of yours by our selfishness, and help us to use them for the good of all men and the glory of your name.

USE OF SCIENCE

Almighty God, from whom alone come insight and understanding: guide and prosper all who are engaged in scientific study and research; that through them knowledge may be increased and the life of mankind may be enriched; through Jesus Christ our Lord.

Lord, we have found out so much knowledge
    and yet possess so little wisdom:
we pray that in your mercy
    you will save us from ourselves.

Help us to learn the right use of nature
  no less quickly than we unlock her treasures;
and give us hearts and wills made new in Christ
  to dedicate your gifts of knowledge
to the service of others
  and to the praise of his name.

O God, the giver of wisdom, who in the beginning made man to have dominion over the works of your hands: grant that with every increase of knowledge and of power we may seek to render further service to mankind, and so to set forward the purpose of your love made known to us in Jesus Christ our Lord.

DAILY WORK AND INDUSTRY

ALMIGHTY God, Father of all mankind, we pray for those engaged in the industries and commerce of this land. Defend them from injustice and oppression, that they may receive the due reward of their labours; and deepen within them the spirit of humble and unselfish service, that they may live and work together for the common good; through Jesus Christ our Lord.

Give, O Lord, to all who work in the field and on the land wisdom to understand and obey your laws; that the harvests of the earth may be neither hoarded nor squandered, but that all may share abundantly in the fruits of the soil, for the honour of your name.

We ask your blessing, our Father, on those whose work lies in their homes. Give them patience, love and a cheerful spirit, and inspire them with the knowledge that in ministering to others they are serving the Lord Christ.

O God, Creator of all things, who made man in your image so that he might find his joy and fulfilment in all that he does: help us so to order our common life that all who are unemployed may have work to do and gain satisfaction in doing it; through Jesus Christ our Lord.

ANIMALS

FATHER in heaven, we thank you for all living things which you have made, and especially for animals. Give to all who deal with them a heart of compassion, that no dumb creature may suffer cruelty or fear at our hands; and keep us always thankful for their faithful companionship and service; through Jesus Christ our Lord.

FOR THE DAY

HEAVENLY Father, in whom we live and move and have our being, we pray that you will so guide and govern us by your Holy Spirit that in all the cares and occupations of our daily life we may never forget you, but remember that we are always walking in your sight; through Christ our Lord.

A collect

ALMIGHTY and everlasting God, mercifully look upon our infirmities, and in all our dangers and necessities stretch forth thy right hand to help and defend us; through Jesus Christ our Lord.

HYMN

THE BLESSING

4

THE LOVE OF GOD

God is love, and he who abides in love abides in God, and God abides in him.

Herein is love, not that we loved God, but that he loved us.

O LORD, whose mercy reaches to the heavens, whose faithfulness knows no end: let the greatness of your love be known to us, that we may worship you with wonder, joy and thanksgiving.

HYMN

WE praise you, God the Father Almighty, Maker of heaven and earth, because your love and faithfulness never fail.

We praise you, Lord Jesus Christ, Son of God, Saviour of the world, for you have won life for us through your passion and victory.

We praise you, God the Holy Spirit, Lord and Life-giver, for you are with us always to guide and to strengthen us and to lead us into the truth.

Most merciful and eternal God, Father, Son, and Holy Spirit, we give you praise and glory for ever and ever.

OUR FATHER...

CANTICLE OR PSALM

BIBLE READING

HEAVENLY Father, we have known and believed the love you have for us.

May we, by dwelling in love, dwell in you, and you in us.

So fashion us after your own way of love, and so shed that love abroad in our hearts by the Holy Spirit, that we may abound in love, to the glory of your name.

Most merciful Father, who through your Son Jesus Christ gave us a new commandment that we should love one another: give us also grace that we may fulfil it. Make us gentle, courteous and forbearing; and so direct our lives that we may look each to the good of others in word and deed; for his sake who loved us and gave himself for us, Jesus Christ our Lord.

A collect

O GOD, who hast prepared for them that love thee such good things as pass man's understanding: pour into our hearts such love toward thee, that we, loving thee above all things, may obtain thy promises, which exceed all that we can desire; through Jesus Christ our Lord.

THE MINISTRY OF HEALING

HEAVENLY Father, giver of life and health, look in your mercy on the sick and suffering; that by your blessing upon them, and upon those who minister to them, they may be restored if it be your will to health of body and mind; through Jesus Christ our Lord.

Lord Jesus Christ, in the days of your flesh
    the sick were brought to you that you might heal
        them:
hear us as we now bring to you in our prayers
    those who are ill, in body or in mind.

May your presence be with them
    to relieve suffering and distress
and to restore them to fullness of life,
    for your name's sake.

THE INCURABLE

HEAVENLY Father, to whom the needs of every heart are known, let the cry of your children come to you; and look in mercy on all who are beyond human help, all whose hope is gone, all whose sickness finds no cure. Give them your strength, O God, to endure with courage and patience, and let your presence dispel all fear; through Jesus Christ our Lord.

Almighty God, whose grace is sufficient
    for all our need,
and whose power comes to full strength
    in our weakness:
we pray for all who suffer
    and who never get well,
that sustained in their weakness
    and released from pain,
they may rejoice in the power of Christ
    resting upon them.
We ask this in his name.

FAMILY LIFE

FATHER in heaven, pattern of all parenthood and lover of children, we pray for homes and families across the world.

Sustain and comfort them in need and sorrow.

In times of bitterness, tension and division, draw near to heal.

May parents and children together be learners in the

school of Christ, daily increasing in mutual respect and understanding, in tolerance and patience, and in all-prevailing love; through Jesus Christ our Lord.

Heavenly Father, from whom every family
   in heaven and on earth is named:
we entrust to your love and care
   the members of our families wherever they may be.
Supply their needs and guide their steps;
   keep them in safety of body and soul;
and let your peace rest upon us all,
   for Jesus Christ's sake.

IN OLD AGE

ETERNAL God, we rejoice in your promise that as our day is, so shall our strength be; and we ask your help for all who are old and wearied with the burden of life. In your strength may they find courage and peace; and in their advancing years may they learn more of your love; through Jesus Christ our Lord.

FOR THE DAY

HELP us, O God, to live today in such a way that we may show our gratitude for all the blessings you have given us; through Jesus Christ our Lord.

You have shown us, O Lord, what is good.
Enable us to perform what you require:
   to do justly,
   to love mercy,
   and to walk humbly with you,
our Father and our God.

HYMN

THE BLESSING

5

THE WORD MADE FLESH

The Word was made flesh and dwelt among us; and we beheld his glory full of grace and truth.

The Lord has visited and redeemed us. O come, let us adore him.

LORD God, our heavenly Father, who for love of our fallen race sent your Son to dwell among us, full of grace and truth: we give you our thanks, we worship and adore you.

HYMN

ETERNAL God, who through long ages
prepared the way for the coming of Christ:
we praise you for your word through the prophets
    who spoke in your name,
and for all the experience and discipline of life
    that made the world long for a Saviour.
We praise you that when the time was ready Jesus came,
    as Man among men,
    as Saviour from sin,
    as Lord of life,
    and Conqueror of death.
Help us to welcome him into our lives,
    and into the life of the world,
and so to praise you more,
    now and in all the time to come.

OUR FATHER...

CANTICLE OR PSALM

BIBLE READING

LORD Jesus Christ, in all the fullness of your power most gentle, in your exceeding greatness most humble: bestow your mind and spirit on us, who have nothing of which to boast; that clothed in true humility we may be exalted to true greatness, for the glory of your name.

> We give thanks to God our Father
> for the gift of his Son to be our Saviour;
> for the love of Christ in taking our human nature;
> for his lowly birth at Bethlehem;
> and for the great redemption he has brought to us and
> to all mankind.
> And with the angelic host we too would cry,
> Glory to God in the highest,
> and on earth peace, goodwill towards men.

Lord Jesus Christ, you have revealed yourself to us, and in this way have revealed your Father also. But our minds and hearts are slow to believe and love. Open us, Lord, to the wonder of your manhood; stir us to the following of your example; urge us to the realisation of your life here on earth in terms of our living, that we may truly live for our fellow human beings, and so live for you, our God for ever and ever.

THE CHURCH, THE BODY OF CHRIST

> HEAVENLY Father, who formed your church
> to be the Body of Christ
> and the instrument of his saving purpose on earth:

cleanse and renew its life
   in the world of our day,
and make it a living fellowship of the Spirit
   to spread your good news
   and to serve mankind,
for the glory of your name.

A collect

ALMIGHTY and everlasting God, by whose Spirit the whole body of the Church is governed and sanctified: receive our supplications and prayers, which we offer before thee for all estates of men in thy holy Church, that every member of the same, in his vocation and ministry, may truly and godly serve thee; through our Lord and Saviour Jesus Christ.

CHRISTIAN UNITY

ETERNAL God, look mercifully upon the broken body of your Church. Draw its members into closer fellowship one with another by the bands of your love; that its restored unity may bring healing to the nations and advance the kingdom of our Lord Jesus Christ.

Heavenly Father, in your word you have taught us to maintain the unity of the Spirit in the bond of peace:

forgive our complacency with the present divisions in your Church.

Break down the barriers of pride and misunderstanding which keep us and our fellow Christians apart.

Make us more humble and deepen our love one for another; and show us how we can more closely worship and work together as members of the one Body of Christ our Lord.

PEACE ON EARTH

ETERNAL God, Lord of men and nations, cleanse our hearts from the bitterness, envy, suspicion and fear which breed strife. May we never think or speak of those nations from which we differ except as fellow human beings who, with us, stand in need of your mercy; and give to us all the wisdom we need to build a world of righteousness and peace.

O God, to whom glory is sung in the highest while on earth peace is proclaimed to men of goodwill: grant that goodwill to us your servants, and send forth the spirit of peace into the hearts of all your people; through Jesus Christ our Lord.

FOR THE DAY

GOD our Father, so fill us this day with the grace of our Lord Jesus Christ that all our thoughts and words and deeds may be acceptable in your sight, and our lives may do honour to your name.

Forgive us, Lord, our shallow pleasures and self-centred joys. Save us from apathy and sleep of soul. Teach us to love life and labour before rest and ease, and to seek contentment only in your will; through Jesus Christ our Lord.

HYMN

THE BLESSING

6

JESUS CHRIST OUR LORD

Jesus said, Come unto me, all ye that labour and are heavy laden, and I will give you rest.

Seek ye the Lord while he may be found; call ye upon him while he is near.

LORD Christ, holy and strong, holy and immortal: God from God, Light from Light, born of a woman, crucified, risen, ascended: receive our adoration, our homage, and our love.

HYMN

GLORY to God in the highest,
and peace to his people on earth.
Lord God, heavenly King,
almighty God and Father,
   we worship you, we give you thanks,
   we praise you for your glory.
Lord Jesus Christ, only Son of the Father,
Lord God, Lamb of God,
you take away the sin of the world:
   have mercy upon us;
you are seated at the right hand of the Father:
   receive our prayer.
For you alone are the Holy One,
you alone are the Lord,
you alone are the Most High,
   Jesus Christ, with the Holy Spirit,
   in the glory of God the Father.

OUR FATHER...

CANTICLE OR PSALM

BIBLE READING

LORD Christ, true Word of God and revelation of the Father: come and take possession of our hearts and reign where you have the right to reign; and so fill our minds and imaginations with the picture of your love that there may be no room in us for any desire discordant with your will, for the glory of your name.

Come, Lord Jesus, and reign over us
as our rightful King.
Rule in our hearts
and fill them with your love.
Rule in our minds
and bring every thought into captivity to yourself.
Rule in our lives
and make them holy like your own.
For yours is the kingdom and the power and the glory,
for ever.

O Lord God, keep ever in our remembrance the life and death of our Saviour Jesus Christ. Make the thought of his love powerful to win us from evil; and as he toiled and sorrowed and suffered for us in fighting against sin, so may we endure constantly as his soldiers and servants, and be partakers of his conflict, his cross, and his victory.

THE SERVICE OF MANKIND

LORD Jesus Christ, whose days on earth were spent in serving others, give to your people a mind to do the same. Take from our hearts all pride and love of power,

that in your service we may find our freedom and our joy.
For your name's sake.

Heavenly Father, whose Son Jesus Christ declared to his
disciples, I am among you as one who serves: take from us
the spirit of selfishness and deepen within us the spirit of
service; that we may think less of our own interests and
more of the needs of others, after the example of our Lord.

Son of Man, you took the form of a servant
    and gave yourself for others.
Fill us with your own spirit of love and service,
    and teach us to see you in all who suffer,
that we may serve them gladly and unselfishly,
    and all for your sake, our Saviour and our Lord.

THE COMING OF CHRIST'S KINGDOM

MAKE yourself known, O Lord Christ, throughout the
world which you died to save.
Reveal yourself among all nations, amid all peoples, and
across all barriers.
Renew your Church with love and power, that the
kingdoms of this world may become your own and all may
acknowledge you to be the Lord, to the glory of God the
Father.

THE HOMELESS AND REFUGEES

LORD Jesus Christ, born in a stable, hear the cry of the
homeless and refugees; and so move our wills by your
Holy Spirit that we may not rest content until all have
found home and livelihood, for your name's sake.

God and Father of us all, whose Son Jesus Christ
    lived as the Son of Man with nowhere to lay his head:
We pray for the millions who are without a home,
    without security,
    and often without hope;
and we ask that through the service
    of all who can help them
their needs may be met
    and a new day of joy and opportunity may be theirs;
through Jesus Christ our Lord.

FOR THE DAY

WE pray, our Father, that you will so deepen our understanding that we may be able to enter with sympathy into the joys and sorrows of others, and so to strengthen and cheer their hearts; through Jesus Christ our Lord.

A collect

STIR up, we beseech thee, O Lord, the wills of thy faithful people; that they, plenteously bringing forth the fruit of good works, may of thee be plenteously rewarded; through Jesus Christ our Lord.

HYMN

THE BLESSING

7

THE WAY, THE TRUTH, AND THE LIFE

I am the way, the truth, and the life; no one comes to the Father but by me.

Draw near to God, and he will draw near to you.

LORD Jesus Christ, you declared yourself to be the way, the truth, and the life. Reveal to us your truth and inspire us with your life, that now and at all times we may find in you the way to the Father.

HYMN

FATHER, we thank you that you so loved the world
that in the fullness of time
    you sent your only Son to be our Saviour.
He was conceived through the power of the Holy Spirit
and born of the Virgin Mary,
    a man like us in all things but sin.
To the poor he proclaimed the good news of salvation,
to prisoners, freedom,
    to those in sorrow, joy.
In fulfilment of your will
he gave himself up to death;
but by rising from the dead
    he destroyed death and restored life.
And that we might live no longer for ourselves
but for him,
he sent the Holy Spirit from you, Father,
as his first gift to those who believe,
to complete his work on earth
    and bring us the fullness of grace.

Therefore, O God, we give you thanks and glory,
   now and for evermore.

OUR FATHER . . .

CANTICLE OR PSALM

BIBLE READING

O LIVING God, in whom is the fountain of life, so teach
  us to know you through your Son Jesus Christ that
we may share the power of that eternal life which is in him,
and our lives may be brought into harmony with his will.

Lord Christ, image of the invisible God,
   in whom are hidden all the treasures of wisdom
   and knowledge:
lead us out of the darkness of our ignorance
   into the light of your truth,
and direct our lives into the way of peace,
   for your name's sake.

A prayer of Erasmus

O LORD Jesus Christ,
  who art the way, the truth, and the life:
   suffer us not to stray from thee, who art the way,
   nor to distrust thee, who art the truth,
   nor to rest in any other thing than thee, who art
    the life.
Teach us by thy Holy Spirit
   what to believe,
   what to do,
   and wherein to take our rest.

RULERS AND STATESMEN

LORD God, we pray that your Holy Spirit may rest on all who bear responsibility for government among the nations. Give them wisdom, courage and strength, that they may make and maintain a true and lasting peace, and that the peoples of the world may dwell together without enmity and without fear, to the glory of your name.

O God, the Lord of all kings and kingdoms, let your strong hand control the nations and cause them to long for your love to rule on the earth.

Strengthen the hands of all who are working for righteousness and peace.

Guide the minds of rulers and statesmen, that they may seek the establishment of justice and freedom for all peoples, both small and great; through Jesus Christ our Lord.

Almighty God, we pray for those who occupy high office in the nations of the world: help them to govern wisely and well; to seek the welfare of all their people; and to make their contribution to the stability, well-being and peace of the world.

EDUCATION

HEAVENLY Father, we pray for those who are responsible for the upbringing and education of children; that both parents and teachers may be able to give them a desire to explore the world of knowledge, a sense of the wonder of life, and the ability to embrace what is good and to reject what is evil; through Jesus Christ our Lord.

Lord Jesus Christ, perfect teacher of men,
   we pray for those who educate the young.
Inspire them with your concern for every part of life,
   that the goal of learning may be maturity and
     fulfilment
in lives dedicated to the service of your kingdom.

TRAVELLERS

WE commend to your keeping, our Father, those who travel by land or sea or air. Give them your protection on the way, enfold them in your peace, and bring them safely to their journey's end; through Jesus Christ our Lord.

Almighty God, give to us and to all who use the roads the spirit of courtesy and goodwill, of carefulness and self-control; that by our thought for others we may all be preserved from needless danger and sudden death, and may live to glorify your name in our going out and in our coming in.

THOSE WE LOVE

FATHER of mercies, we bring to you in our prayers all whom we love, knowing that your love for them is greater than ours and that you will for them only what is for their good. So have them in your keeping, O Lord, and give them now and always the blessing of your peace; for Jesus Christ's sake.

FOR THE DAY

LORD God, increase in us the spirit of courage, that we may go forth with hopeful spirits to the duties of this day, confident that with your help we can fashion something good from whatever the day may bring.

A collect

ASSIST us mercifully, O Lord, in these our supplications and prayers, and dispose the way of thy servants towards the attainment of everlasting salvation; that, among all the changes and chances of this mortal life, they may ever be defended by thy most gracious and ready help; through Jesus Christ our Lord.

HYMN

THE BLESSING

8

CHRIST CRUCIFIED

God forbid that I should glory, save in the cross of our Lord Jesus Christ.

Behold, the Lamb of God, who takes away the sin of the world.

If any man will follow me, let him deny himself and take up his cross and follow me.

WE adore you, O Christ, and we praise you because by your cross and passion you have redeemed the world.

HYMN

HOLY Lord God, you did not spare your own Son but gave him up for us all.
We remember his obedience to your will,
    even to the death of the cross.
We remember his forgiveness of those who crucified
    him and nailed him to the cruel tree.
We rejoice in his love for the world
    which nothing could destroy.
We rejoice in his victory over all evil
    and the power of death.
Holy Lord God, have mercy upon us
    whom you reconciled to yourself through your Son.

OUR FATHER...

CANTICLE OR PSALM

BIBLE READING

A collect

ALMIGHTY God, we beseech thee graciously to behold this thy family, for which our Lord Jesus Christ was contented to be betrayed, and given up into the hands of wicked men, and to suffer death upon the cross, who now liveth and reigneth with thee and the Holy Spirit, ever one God, world without end.

Almighty and everlasting God,
  whose Son our Saviour Jesus Christ
triumphed in death on the cross
  that he might win life for the world:
help us in the power of his victory
  to triumph over all evil
  and to glory in his cross alone;
who is alive and reigns with you and the Holy Spirit,
  one God for ever and ever.

Lord Jesus, we praise you for your redeeming love
  and all that you have done for us.
As we bow in penitence before the cross
  we gratefully acknowledge the debt we owe.
For ours was the sin you bore,
  ours the ransom you paid,
  ours the salvation you won.
Lord Jesus, accept our thanksgiving
  and make us more worthy of your love,
  for your love's sake.

We confess to you, our Father, how often we shirk the cross and try to avoid the discipline and pain of self-surrender; how often we fail to see the cross in the needs and sufferings of others; how often we deny the cross by asserting instead of giving ourselves. Grant us the courage to die to self, so that we may live for others and find in them a meeting place with you.

RECONCILIATION

HEAVENLY Father, you have reconciled the world to yourself through the cross of your Son and have committed to your Church the ministry of reconciliation: grant that we who bear witness to your reconciling word with our lips may also show your reconciling power in our lives, that the world may believe, to the glory of your name.

Behold in your mercy, O God, the deep divisions of your world:
    the lack of understanding between nations and classes;
    the privilege and pride of the strong,
    the envy and resentment of the weak.
Set in men's hearts the spirit of penitence, forgiveness and reconciliation, that they may no longer distrust one another but be led into the way of peace; through Jesus Christ our Lord.

THOSE WHO SUFFER

LORD Jesus, by the loneliness of your suffering on the cross be near to all who are desolate and in pain or sorrow this day. May your presence transform their sorrow into comfort, and in fellowship with you may they find peace, for your mercy's sake.

Almighty God, in the name of Jesus your Son,
    who healed the sick and consoled the sad,
we pray for all who suffer
    through sickness of body or mind,
    through fear or depression,
    through loneliness or bereavement;

and we ask that according to your will
   they may be healed and comforted,
for the sake of Jesus Christ our Lord.

FOR PRISONERS

LORD God, we pray for all who have been imprisoned by
their fellow men;

  for those who are in prison for crimes they have committed, that they resolve on a new way of life and find in
you the help they need when they are released;

  for those who are in prison for conscience sake, that they
may stand firm for what they believe to be right and be
sustained with courage and hope.

  We ask this in Christ's name.

FOR THE DAY

O SAVIOUR of the world, who by thy cross and precious
blood hast redeemed us: save us, and help us, we
humbly beseech thee, O Lord.

Prayer of St Richard

THANKS be to you, our Lord Jesus Christ,
  for all the benefits which you have given us,
    for all the pains and insults which you have borne for us.
Most merciful Redeemer, Friend and Brother,
  may we know you more clearly,
  love you more dearly,
  and follow you more nearly,
    day by day.

HYMN

THE BLESSING

9

THE RISEN LORD

The Lord is risen; he is risen indeed.

*I am the first and the last, and the living one;
I died, and behold I am alive for evermore.*

*Thou, O Lord, art in the midst of us, and we are called by
thy name.*

WORTHY is the Lamb who was slain to receive power
and riches, and wisdom and strength, and honour
and glory and blessing.

HYMN

ETERNAL God and Father, by whose power
our Lord Jesus Christ was raised from the dead:
with the whole company of your people in heaven and
    on earth
  we rejoice and give thanks,
that he who was dead is alive again
  and lives for evermore;
that he is with us now and always,
  and that nothing can part us from your love in him;
that he has opened the way to your kingdom
  and brought us the gift of eternal life.
All glory, praise and thanksgiving,
  all worship, honour and love,
be yours, almighty and everlasting God,
  in time and for all eternity.

OUR FATHER...

CANTICLE OR PSALM

BIBLE READING

O GOD, who by the resurrection of your Son Jesus Christ from the dead delivered us from the power of darkness and brought us into the kingdom of your love: grant that as by his death he has recalled us to life, so by his presence ever abiding in us he may raise us to joys eternal.

Almighty God, we praise you for the resurrection of your Son our Lord and for his triumph over death and the grave; and we ask you so to raise us with Christ to newness of life that we may serve you in the power and joy of his resurrection; through the same Jesus Christ our Lord.

A collect

O GOD, who for our redemption didst give thy only begotten Son to the death of the cross, and by his glorious resurrection hast delivered us from the power of the enemy: grant us so to die daily unto sin, that we may evermore live with him in the joy of his resurrection; through the same Jesus Christ our Lord.

ALL DEPARTED SOULS

HELP us, O God, to trust you not for ourselves alone, but for those also whom we love and who are hid from us by the shadow of death; that as we believe your power to have raised our Lord Jesus Christ from the dead, so we may trust your love to give eternal life to all who believe in him, who is the resurrection and the life.

O Lord our God, whose love holds in its embrace your children in this world and in the next: so unite us to yourself that in fellowship with you we may always be united to our loved ones whether here or there; give us courage, constancy and hope, through him who died and was buried and rose again for us, Jesus Christ our Lord.

O God of infinite goodness and compassion, who gave your Son to die for the sins of the whole world: we rejoice in your love for all creation; and we commend all men, living and departed, to your everlasting mercy, that in them your will may be done, through Jesus Christ our Lord.

THE CHRISTIAN HOPE

ETERNAL God, in whom is all our hope in life, in death, and to all eternity: grant that, rejoicing in the eternal life which is ours in Christ, we may face whatever the future holds in store for us calm and unafraid, always confident that neither death nor life can part us from your love in Jesus Christ our Lord.

Christ is alive, the conqueror of all his foes, and ours.
Christ is alive, and in his hands are the keys of death and the unseen world.
Christ is alive, and in him we are born again to a living hope and an eternal inheritance.
We praise you, O Christ, for your resurrection victory.
We acknowledge you as our living Lord and Saviour.
We rejoice in hope of the glory of God.

A collect

GRANT, O Lord, that as we are baptised into the death of thy blessed Son our Saviour Jesus Christ, so by continual mortifying our corrupt affections we may be buried with him; and that, through the grave, and gate of death, we may pass to our joyful resurrection; for his merits, who died, and was buried, and rose again for us, thy Son Jesus Christ our Lord.

THOSE WHO MOURN

GOD of hope and giver of all comfort, we commend to your tender care those who mourn the loss of loved ones. Give them the peace that passes all understanding, and make them to know that neither death nor life can separate them from your love in Jesus Christ our Lord.

Almighty God, Lord of life and vanquisher of death, we praise you for the sure hope of eternal life you have given us in the resurrection of our Lord Jesus Christ; and we pray that all who mourn the loss of those dear to them may enter into his victory and know his peace; for his name's sake.

FOR THE DAY

RECEIVE into your keeping, O God, ourselves and all those we love, and teach us in life and death to put our trust in you, our strength and our redeemer.

Risen Lord, who on the first Easter day drew near your two disciples on the Emmaus road, and at evening stayed with them in their village home: be our unseen companion along the daily journey of our life, and at the ending of the day come and abide with us in our dwellings; for your love's sake.

HYMN

THE BLESSING

10

THE KING OF KINGS

The kingdom of the world has become the kingdom of our Lord and of his Christ; and he shall reign for ever and ever.

I would find thee, whom no eye can see; only the heart can rise and reach thy throne above the skies.

We see Jesus, who was made lower than the angels, crowned with glory and honour.

O CHRIST, you are the King of glory,
   you are the Father's everlasting Son.
When you had vanquished the sting of death,
you opened the kingdom of heaven to all
      who believe in you.
You sit at the right hand of God
   in the glory of the Father.

HYMN

CHRIST has ascended up on high
   and reigns on the throne of the universe,
      crowned with glory and honour.
For God has highly exalted him and bestowed on him
   the name which is above every name.
He must reign until he has put
   all his enemies under his feet.

Lord Christ, we acknowledge your kingship,
   we worship and adore you.
Accept our homage, come and reign over us,
   and extend your empire over all the world,

that every tongue may confess you Lord,
to the glory of God the Father.

OUR FATHER...

CANTICLE OR PSALM

BIBLE READING

ALMIGHTY God, whose Son our Saviour Jesus Christ ascended far above all heavens that he might fill all things: grant that your Church on earth may be filled with his presence, and that he may remain with us always, even to the end of the world.

Christ is the King
to whom all authority has been given
in heaven and on earth.
      We own him as our Lord.
      We yield him our obedience.
      We dedicate our lives to his service.
Come, Lord Christ, and reign in us,
and make us the agents of your kingdom in the world.

A collect

O LORD, the King of glory, who through the eternal gates didst ascend to thy Father's throne: grant that, while thou dost reign in heaven, we may not be bowed down to the things of earth, but that our hearts may be lifted up whither thou, our redemption, art gone before; who with the Father and the Holy Spirit livest and reignest, ever one God, world without end.

THE KINGDOM OF CHRIST

O GLORIOUS Christ, who in your ascension entered into your kingdom: remember the millions who have not heard of the redemption you have won for them.

Grant that they may learn, through your Church, of the new and living way which you have opened for them.

So may they draw near in fullness of faith and enter with you into the Father's presence, and receive forgiveness and peace.

Come, Lord Jesus, and deliver your creation from corruption into the glorious liberty of the children of God.

Come and destroy the evil which is yet triumphant in the world.

Come with your life-giving Spirit and make all things new.

Even so, come, Lord Jesus.

THE QUEEN

A LMIGHTY God, the fountain of all goodness, we humbly beseech thee to bless our gracious Queen Elizabeth, Elizabeth the Queen Mother, Philip, Duke of Edinburgh, Charles, Prince of Wales, and all the Royal Family. Endue them with thy Holy Spirit; enrich them with thy heavenly grace; prosper them with all happiness; and bring them to thine everlasting kingdom; through Jesus Christ our Lord.

O GOD, who providest for thy people by thy power, and rulest over them in love: vouchsafe so to bless thy servant Elizabeth our Queen, that under her this nation may be wisely governed, and thy Church may serve thee in all godly quietness; through Jesus Christ our Lord.

SOCIAL JUSTICE

Holy Spirit, fountain of light and truth, help us to understand the causes of our social tensions and unrest. Open our eyes to economic wrongs and racial bias; deepen our concern for the old, the poor, and the handicapped; and stir in us all a burning sense of responsibility one for another, as servants of Jesus Christ our Lord.

O God, the King of righteousness,
    lead us in the ways of justice and peace.
Inspire us to break down all injustice and oppression,
    to gain for every man his due reward,
    and from every man his due service;
that each may live for all,
    and all may care for each,
for the sake of Jesus Christ our Lord.

FOR THE DAY

Give us, O God, this day quiet and confident hearts, that we may go on our way with courage and with hope, through the grace of our Lord Jesus Christ.

Lord, take our minds and think through them;
take our lips and speak through them;
take our hearts and set them on fire with love
    for Christ and his kingdom.

HYMN

THE BLESSING

II

THE PRINCE OF PEACE

Peace I leave with you; my peace I give to you.
Let not your hearts be troubled, neither let them
be afraid.

Thou wilt keep him in perfect peace, whose mind
is stayed on thee.

A collect

ALMIGHTY God, teach us to live as ever in your presence, that we may abide in your peace all the days of our life; through Jesus Christ our Lord.

HYMN

O LORD our God, whose reconciling love and power have been declared to us in the death and resurrection of our Saviour Jesus Christ:

keep us ever mindful of the price you have paid for the salvation of the world.

Let the cross of your Son bear in us its fruits of love and righteousness and peace.

Help us to share his holy indignation in the presence of evil, and his merciful compassion for those who commit it.

And teach us to forgive one another, since we ourselves live only in your forgiveness, which is ours through Jesus Christ our Lord.

OUR FATHER...

CANTICLE OR PSALM

BIBLE READING

WE give thanks, our Father, for those who amid life's anxieties and disappointments remain serene and strong, confident that their journey here is a pilgrimage and not a meaningless voyage into the unknown. Help us, by their example of cheerfulness and courage, to believe that every experience presents us with an opportunity of increasing wisdom, and that every ending passes into a new beginning; through Jesus Christ our Lord.

Prayer of St Francis

LORD, make us instruments of your peace.
Grant that we may seek
    not so much to be consoled as to console;
    not so much to be understood as to understand;
    not so much to be loved as to love.
For it is in giving that we receive,
    it is in pardoning that we are pardoned,
    it is in dying that we are born again to life eternal.

A collect

O GOD, who art the author of peace and lover of concord, in knowledge of whom standeth our eternal life, whose service is perfect freedom: defend us thy humble servants in all assaults of our enemies; that we, surely trusting in thy defence, may not fear the power of any adversaries; through the might of Jesus Christ our Lord.

THE PEACE OF THE WORLD

ALMIGHTY God, King and Judge of all mankind, look in pity upon the nations oppressed by strife, bitterness and fear.

We acknowledge our share in the sins which have brought us so often to the brink of destruction.

May your goodness lead us to repentance, that we may yet be spared.

Restrain the pride, the passions and the follies of men, and grant us your grace, mercy and peace, through Jesus Christ our Saviour.

Grant, Lord, for the sake of those whose lives were lost in war, and for the sake of the generations to come, that the nations of the world may learn your way of peace; and that all men may have a chance to enjoy the life you have given them, free from war, tyranny and oppression.

THE FORCES OF THE CROWN

O GOD our Father, we pray for all who serve our country as sailors, soldiers and airmen. Grant that meeting danger with courage, and all occasions with discipline and loyalty, they may truly serve the cause of justice and peace, for the honour of your name.

O God, by whose wisdom and power the wrath of man is turned to your praise: overrule the passions and designs of men, that your kingdom of peace may prevail on earth; and grant that the men and women in the armed forces may serve their nation with constancy, discipline and courage; through Jesus Christ our Lord.

THE CHURCH'S MINISTRY OF PEACE

ALMIGHTY God, give to your Church the unity of the Spirit in the bond of peace; that in the midst of the world she may be the messenger of your grace and pardon; and hasten the day when all races shall unite to praise your name, through Jesus Christ our Lord.

Grant, O God, that your Church may increasingly become a reconciling force among the peoples:

witnessing to the unity of all men in the family of one
Father;
checking passion in time of strife;
reminding men of the ways of Christ;
and exhibiting above all things that brotherhood of
mankind taught by our Master,
Jesus Christ our Lord.

A PRAYER FOR UNITY

O GOD, the Father of our Lord Jesus Christ, our only
Saviour, the Prince of Peace: give us grace seriously
to lay to heart the great dangers we are in by our unhappy
divisions. Take away all hatred and prejudice, and whatso-
ever else may hinder us from godly union and concord;
that, as there is but one body, and one Spirit, and one hope
of our calling, one Lord, one faith, one baptism, one God
and Father of us all, so we may henceforth be all of one
heart and of one soul, united in one holy bond of truth
and peace, of faith and charity, and may with one mind and
one mouth glorify thee; through Jesus Christ our Lord.

FOR THE DAY

ALMIGHTY and everlasting God, who dost govern all
things in heaven and earth: mercifully hear the supplications of thy people, and grant us thy peace all the days of
our life; through Jesus Christ our Lord.

O Lord our God, let your peace be upon us your servants,
that in the doing of your will we may ourselves find peace,
and ever be ministers of peace to others; through Jesus
Christ our Lord.

HYMN

THE BLESSING

12

THE GRACE OF OUR LORD JESUS CHRIST

You know the grace of our Lord Jesus Christ, that though he was rich, yet for our sakes he became poor, that we through his poverty might become rich.

Behold, I stand at the door and knock. If any man open the door, I will come in.

BLESSED be the Lord of heaven and earth, for he has visited and redeemed his people, and has caused the light of the glorious gospel of Christ, who is the image of God, to shine throughout the world.

HYMN

WE bow our knees to the Father, from whom every family in heaven and on earth is named:

that he would grant us, according to the riches of his glory, to be strengthened with power through his Spirit in our inner being;

that Christ may dwell in our hearts by faith; so that we, being rooted and grounded in love, may be strong to comprehend with all the saints what is the breadth and length and height and depth of the love of Christ, which passes knowledge;

that we may be filled with all the fullness of God.

To him be the glory in the Church and in Christ Jesus to all generations, for ever and ever.

OUR FATHER...

CANTICLE OR PSALM

BIBLE READING

LORD Jesus Christ, you came to set at liberty those who are oppressed; and we are oppressed by the tyranny of our guilt and of our fears.

Hear our cry. Forgive our sins. Deliver us from evil.

Teach us to find our freedom in your service, until at last we are free from bondage to the passing things of earth and enjoy the glorious liberty of the children of God, for the glory of your name.

Lord, open our hearts to receive your gift of grace,
the love that releases us from our bondage and gives us
freedom:
freedom from cares and worries that stifle our
happiness;
freedom from sins that cling to us, and to which
we cling;
freedom from all that prevents our becoming what
we can be and ought to be.
So bring us, O Lord, to the experience of life more
abundant,
for your name's sake.

A collect

WE beseech thee, O Lord, to pour thy grace into our hearts; that, as we have known the incarnation of thy Son Jesus Christ by the message of an angel, so by his cross and passion we may be brought to the glory of his resurrection; through the same Jesus Christ our Lord.

MEMBERS OF CHRIST'S CHURCH

O GOD, you have taught us that we are members one of another in the body of Christ: teach us to use wisely and generously the gifts you have given us and to care for each other's needs; that we may live and work together in unity and love, for the glory of Christ our Lord.

We pray, O Lord, for your Church, that all its members may indeed be one body, holding one faith, proclaiming one truth, and following one Lord in holiness of living and love, even your Son our Saviour Jesus Christ.

Merciful God, bless your Church and make all its members sound in faith and holy in life; that they may serve the needs of others and advance the kingdom of our Lord Jesus Christ.

THE CHURCH'S WITNESS

O LORD Jesus Christ, you have commanded us to make known the good news of your love to all nations: help us so to experience your forgiveness, grace and peace that we may want all other people to share those blessings and to come into the family of the one Father, to whom be all gratitude, love and praise for ever and ever.

Lord God our Father,
    you have called your Church
to bear witness to Christ
    as Lord and Saviour of all:
help it so to live in the power of the Spirit
    that the whole world may be turned to you and
    be saved;
through Jesus Christ our Lord.

We commend to your mercy, O God, our fellow Christians who bear their witness for Christ in places of conflict, and all who suffer for the gospel's sake. Uphold their faith and give them grace to endure, that your kingdom may be advanced and your Church strengthened by adversity; through Jesus Christ our Lord.

FOR THE DAY

GIVE us, O Lord, so firm a faith in your fatherly love and wisdom that we may be lifted above our anxieties and fears, and face the life of each day, and all the unknown future, with a courageous and quiet spirit.

Prayer of St Ignatius Loyola

TEACH us, good Lord, to serve thee as thou deservest:
to give, and not to count the cost;
to fight, and not to heed the wounds;
to toil, and not to seek for rest;
to labour, and not to ask for any reward save that
of knowing that we do thy will;
through Jesus Christ our Lord.

HYMN

THE BLESSING

13

LORD AND LIFE-GIVER

God is a spirit, and they that worship him must worship him in spirit and in truth.

You are the temple of God, and the Spirit of God dwelleth in you.

Spirit of the living God, come and fill the hearts of your servants and kindle within us the fire of your love, that we may worship in spirit and in truth.

HYMN

Spirit of God, present in creation, bringing order out of chaos, giving life to all things and sustaining them all in being;
  present at the new creation when the Word was made flesh and Jesus was born;
  present at his baptism and in his life and ministry;
  present with the disciples on the day of Pentecost, and with the servants of Christ at all times;
  present with us now to bring us to faith, to fill us with love, and to unite us in the fellowship of the Church.
Spirit of God, Lord and giver of life,
  we give you praise and glory, now and for ever.

OUR FATHER . . .

CANTICLE OR PSALM

BIBLE READING

O HOLY Spirit of God, by whom all things live and through whom the hearts of men are cleansed and strengthened: guide us in all perplexity, unite us in time of discord, comfort us in sorrow, kindle in us the fire of your love; and so increase in us your gifts that we may be strengthened for the service of our Lord and his kingdom.

Save us, Lord, from sinning against your Holy Spirit.
    May we not grieve the Spirit by living carelessly,
    nor quench the Spirit by our timidity,
    nor resist the Spirit by stubborn disobedience,
but open our lives to his prompting and power, that he may renew us day by day.

A collect

G OD, who didst teach the hearts of thy faithful people by the sending to them the light of thy Holy Spirit: grant us by the same Spirit to have a right judgment in all things, and evermore to rejoice in his holy comfort; through the merits of Christ Jesus our Saviour, who liveth and reigneth with thee, in the unity of the same Spirit, one God, world without end.

THE RENEWAL OF THE CHURCH

H EAVENLY Father, have mercy upon your Church throughout the world. Renew its life, its faith, its worship, its witness; and make it a fit instrument for the furtherance of Christ's kingdom among men, to the honour of his name.

Guide and direct, O Lord, the minds of all who work for the reshaping of the Church in our time.
    Restore our faith and vision.
    Renew our energies and love.

Revive your people to new life and power.

So may we live and speak for Christ before the world he came to save, and ever advance his kingdom.

O most Holy Spirit of God, from whom alone flows the fullness of wisdom and life: come in your everlasting power and glory upon the Church, and into the hearts of men, to bring to the world a new birth of holiness, new understandings of truth, and new unity in love; through Jesus Christ our Lord.

THE CHURCH'S SERVICE

ALMIGHTY God, through whose grace we are called to serve you in the mission of the gospel and in the ministry of your love to all men: bless us with the wisdom and the power of your Spirit, that we may understand your will and be made strong to obey it, for the glory of our Lord Jesus Christ.

Jesus, Lord and Master, teach us and all your people so to follow the pattern of your manhood that we may learn to interpret life in terms of giving, not of getting; to be faithful stewards of our time and talents and all that you have entrusted to us; and to buy up every opportunity of serving the needs of others and advancing your kingdom in the world.

THE MINISTRY OF HEALING

ALMIGHTY God, whose Son our Lord Jesus Christ went about doing good and healing all kinds of illness: continue his gracious work among us today in hospitals and nursing homes. Give wisdom, sympathy and patience to those who minister to the sick; and prosper all that is being done to prevent suffering and to forward the purposes of your love.

Bless, O Lord Christ, all whom you have called to share in your own ministry of healing as doctors and nurses. Give them skill, understanding and compassion, and enable them to do their work in dependence on your grace and for the promotion of your glory.

FOR THE DAY

Heavenly Father, we pray that you will send into our hearts, and into the hearts of all men everywhere, the Spirit of our Lord Jesus Christ.

Defend us, O Lord, with thy heavenly grace, that we may continue thine for ever, and daily increase in thy Holy Spirit more and more, until we come to thy everlasting kingdom.

HYMN

THE BLESSING

14

THE FELLOWSHIP OF THE SPIRIT

By one Spirit we were all baptised into one body, and were all made to drink of one Spirit.

As many as are led by the Spirit of God, they are the sons of God.

O God, we pray that as the Holy Spirit came in wind and fire to the apostles, so he may come to us, breathing life into our souls and kindling in our hearts the flame of love; through Jesus Christ our Lord.

HYMN

HEAVENLY Father, you have taught us that there are
varieties of gifts, but the same Spirit;
that there are varieties of service, but the same Lord;
that there are varieties of working, but it is the same God
    who inspires them all in every one;
that to each is given the manifestation of the Spirit
    for the common good.

We thank you, O God, for the diversity of ministry in your Church; for the things in which we differ as well as for the things in which we are one.

Enlarge our minds to grasp this rich and varied fellowship, that your Church may express in unity all the wealth of that abundant life which is possible in Jesus Christ our Lord.

OUR FATHER...

CANTICLE OR PSALM

BIBLE READING

O LORD Jesus Christ, who prayed for your disciples that they might be one, even as you are one with the Father: draw us to yourself, that in common love and obedience to you we may be united to one another, in the fellowship of the one Spirit, that the world may believe that you are Lord, to the glory of God the Father.

Come, Holy Spirit of God,
   restore the lives which without you are dead;
   kindle the hearts which without you are cold and
      dull;
   enlighten the minds which without you are dark
      and blind;
   fill the Church which without you is an empty
      shrine;
   and teach us how to pray.

O God our Father, bless your Church with unity, peace and concord. Make her here and all over the world a true fellowship of the Spirit in which no distinction is made because of race or colour, class or party; a fellowship of love in which all are really one in Christ. We ask it in his name, who is our one Lord.

PEACE AMONG NATIONS

ALMIGHTY God, without whom all things hasten to destruction: look mercifully upon your family of nations and races, and draw all men into your kingdom of righteousness and truth. Uproot our enmities, heal our divisions, cast out our fears; and renew our faith in your unchanging purpose of goodwill and peace on earth.

> God of righteousness, God of peace,
> forgive the selfishness, greed and arrogance
>   that cause us to be at enmity one with another;
> help us and all men to live together
>   in charity and goodwill;
> and teach the nations of the world
>   the things that belong to their peace;
> through Jesus Christ our Lord.

RACIAL HARMONY

GOD of peace, look in mercy upon the sons of men and increase the spirit of sympathy and understanding between those of different race or colour. Strengthen the love of righteousness and liberty among all people, and bring the whole earth to acknowledge your sovereignty of love and truth; through Jesus Christ our Lord.

Lord God, Creator and Father of us all, you have made of one blood all races and nations of men:

increase among us the spirit of sympathy and understanding, of tolerance and goodwill;

that the prejudices, arrogance and pride which cause division between those of different race or colour may be done away, and all peoples may live together in unity and peace;

through Jesus Christ our Lord.

THE LONELY

WE bring to you in our prayers, heavenly Father, all lonely people, especially those who are too old or infirm to enjoy company, and those who are isolated from others through suffering and pain or through a sense of inferiority. We pray that friends or neighbours may be enabled to reach them and lift them out of their loneliness and bring them comfort and hope. We ask it in Christ's name.

Lord Jesus, friend and brother, bless all who feel isolated and friendless:

the young who have gone from home for the first time to live and work in a big city;

the widow or widower who finds life empty without their life's companion;

the aged who have outgrown their generation and find their family circle very small.

Give to each and all, O Lord, your help, your comfort and your peace.

FOR THE DAY

O GOD, by your Spirit dwelling in our hearts may we know this day the joy of your presence and be given wisdom and strength for every task; through Jesus Christ our Lord.

Lord Jesus Christ, you said to your apostles: I leave you peace, my peace I give you. Look not on our sins, but on the faith of your Church, and grant us the peace and unity of your kingdom, where you live for ever and ever.

HYMN

THE BLESSING

15

THE HOLY TRINITY

*Praise the Lord, O my soul, and all that is within me
praise his holy name.*

*Holy, holy, holy, is the Lord God almighty, who was
and is and is to come.*

ETERNAL Lord God, before the brightness of whose
presence the angels veil their faces: with lowly reverence we acknowledge your infinite glory, Father, Son, and
Holy Spirit, one God, blessed for ever and ever.

HYMN

FATHER, whom we know through your Son Jesus Christ;
Creator of all that is, whose mystery is beyond and
around us, whose love enfolds and seeks us:

Have mercy upon us.

Jesus, son of Mary, born in poverty, sharing our life and
our afflictions; Word of the Father, taking our flesh upon
you; Lamb of God, bearing our sin; Christ triumphant, in
whom is our peace:

Have mercy upon us.

Most Holy Spirit of God, bringing order out of chaos;
Spirit of truth, overcoming falsehood; Spirit of love,
always dwelling in your people; Spirit of life, quickening
our minds and bodies:

Have mercy upon us.

God eternal, Father, Son, and Holy Spirit, from whose presence none can flee, to whose judgment all must come, by whose grace and power we are made whole:

Have mercy upon us.

OUR FATHER...

CANTICLE OR PSALM

BIBLE READING

BLESS us, O God, Father, Son, and Holy Spirit, with the vision of your glory:
that we may know you as the Father who created us,
rejoice in you as the Son who redeemed us,
and be strong in you, the Spirit who sanctifies us.
Keep us steadfast in this faith, and bring us at the last to your eternal kingdom, where you are worshipped and glorified, one God, for ever and ever.

May the strength of God pilot us,
May the power of God preserve us.
May the wisdom of God instruct us.
May the hand of God protect us.
May the way of God direct us.
May the host of God guard us against the snares of the evil one and the temptations of the world.
May Christ be with us, Christ before us, Christ in us, Christ beneath us, Christ over us.
May your salvation, O Lord, be ours this day and for evermore.

A collect

OALMIGHTY God, who hast built thy Church upon the foundation of the apostles and prophets, Jesus Christ himself being the head corner-stone: grant us so to be joined together in unity of spirit by their doctrine, that we may be made a holy temple acceptable unto thee; through Jesus Christ our Lord.

SCHOOLS AND COLLEGES

WE offer this prayer, Father, for our schools and colleges:

that those who teach in them may be endowed with the love and understanding we see revealed in the life and example of Jesus Christ;

that children may be guided in the way that leads to the abundant life which Jesus came to bring us all;

that students may accept with gratitude and humility your gifts of mind and the opportunity to use them;

that the Spirit of truth may use their studies to enlarge their understanding of your purpose for mankind, made known in Jesus Christ our Lord.

> Almighty God, you are the source of truth
>   and your Spirit leads us into the truth:
> may all who teach and all who learn
>   in our schools, colleges and universities
> be set free from everything that might hinder
>   their search for the truth;
> and finding truth, may they learn to use it
>   for the good of mankind
>   and for your greater glory.

CHILDREN

GRANT to our children, heavenly Father, this gift above all, that as they grow in knowledge they may grow also in grace, and enter into their heritage of faith in your Son Jesus Christ our Lord.

Have mercy, O God, on all children who are handicapped by poverty or illness, by broken or unhappy homes. Lift from them the burden of misery and fear. Enable all who care for them to minister with tenderness, and to trust always in your power to heal and restore; through Jesus Christ our Lord.

STEWARDSHIP

LORD Jesus Christ, you have taught us that we cannot love God *and* mammon, and that all our possessions are a trust from you. Teach us to be faithful stewards of our time, our talents, and our money, that we may help others and extend your kingdom, for your name's sake.

FOR THE DAY

FATHER, enable us this day to walk trustfully as your children, giving glory to our Lord Jesus Christ and rejoicing in the power of the Holy Spirit.

Heavenly Father, enlighten our minds and strengthen our wills, that we may know what we ought to do, and be strong to do it through the grace of the Holy Spirit, for the glory of Christ our Lord.

HYMN

THE BLESSING

16

THE FATHERHOOD OF GOD
('Our Father in heaven')

Like as a father pitieth his own children, even so is the Lord merciful unto them that fear him.

Behold what manner of love the Father has bestowed upon us, that we should be called children of God.

FATHER in heaven, we lift our hearts to you
in your holiness and majesty,
in your wisdom and power,
in your love and faithfulness.
We worship and adore you.

HYMN

General thanksgiving

ALMIGHTY God, Father of all mercies, we thine unworthy servants do give thee most humble and hearty thanks for all thy goodness and loving-kindness to us, and to all men.

We bless thee for our creation, preservation, and all the blessings of this life; but above all, for thine inestimable love in the redemption of the world by our Lord Jesus Christ; for the means of grace, and for the hope of glory.

And, we beseech thee, give us that due sense of all thy mercies, that our hearts may be unfeignedly thankful, and that we may show forth thy praise, not only with our lips, but in our lives; by giving up ourselves to thy service, and by walking before thee in holiness and righteousness all our days;

through Jesus Christ our Lord, to whom with thee and the Holy Ghost be all honour and glory, world without end.

OUR FATHER...

CANTICLE OR PSALM

BIBLE READING

O GOD our Father, in whose will is our peace: teach us to be anxious for nothing, and when we have done what you have given us to do, to leave the issue to your wisdom. Take from us doubt and mistrust, and help us to know that all things are possible to us through your Son, our Saviour Jesus Christ.

Father in heaven, we thank you for the witness of
    countless men and women
      who have put their trust in you and found unfailing
      power and love.
We pray that your Spirit may give us grace
    when burdened with difficulties, to trust in
      your strength;
    when overwhelmed with sorrow, to rest in your
      love;
    when emptied of feeling and purpose, to know you
      are present;
after the example of our Saviour Jesus Christ,
    who through the utmost suffering of body,
      agony of mind and darkness of soul,
    still trusted in you.

Almighty God, whose fatherly love holds us all in its embrace: we thank you for the many blessings you have lavished upon us your children.

We confess that we have so often misused your gifts, marred your work, and proved unworthy of your love.

Have mercy upon us, O God; forgive us our sins, and teach us to walk in the ways of your family; through Jesus Christ our Lord.

BROTHERHOOD AND PEACE

O GOD, whose purpose of love enfolds the whole world, send peace upon earth, that the nations may no longer prepare for war, and that they may seek not to destroy but to understand one another. Take away all bitterness and hatred, and grant that people of all colours and races may learn to live in fellowship together; through Jesus Christ our Lord.

O God, Father of all mankind,
    fill us with your love and understanding,
that in all our dealings one with another
    we may exercise mercy,
and show forth our brotherhood in your Son,
    Jesus Christ our Lord.

Heavenly Father, we thank you for bringing us into the family of your Church through our Lord Jesus Christ.

We pray that we, and all who call themselves by his name, may be led into ways of co-operation and mutual understanding.

Help us to work together in your strength, that we may serve you more truly and witness more effectively to your love for all men.

FAMILY LIFE

GOD our Father, be with us in our homes through this and every day. Help us, when we are tired, to control our wills and tempers and to take thought for others. Make us loving and patient, forgiving others as we hope to be forgiven; that in our homes your royal law of love may reign; through Jesus Christ our Lord.

God our Father, whose Son Jesus Christ
    lived at Nazareth as a member of a human family:
hear our prayer for all homes and families,
    and especially for our own,
that they may be blessed by his presence
    and united in his love.

REFUGEES

GOD and Father of all, we ask your mercy
    for the refugees of many nations.
We pray for the sick, the homeless and the lonely,
    and for those separated from family and friends.
Direct the minds of statesmen,
    and the charity of all men,
to the relief of their sufferings and the healing of
        their sorrows;
    through Jesus Christ our Lord.

You have awakened us, Lord God, to the hunger of millions of our fellow men, and to the great difference between their lives and our own. Help us to see clearly what you require of us, alike in the giving of aid as in the renouncing of privilege, and not to shrink from the sacrifice involved, as we ask it in Christ's name.

FOR THE DAY

HEAVENLY Father, whose love is unchanging and unchangeable: enable us to trust you so fully that we may be set free from anxiety, and may find both strength for our tasks and peace in doing them; through Jesus Christ our Lord.

A collect

O GOD, forasmuch as without thee we are not able to please thee: mercifully grant that thy Holy Spirit may in all things direct and rule our hearts; through Jesus Christ our Lord.

HYMN

THE BLESSING

17

THE HOLINESS OF GOD
('Hallowed be your name')

Give the Lord the honour due unto his name: worship the Lord with holy worship. Amen, Amen.

Unto thee, O Lord, do I lift up my soul: my God, I trust in thee.

LOOK graciously upon us, O Holy Spirit, and give us, for our hallowing, thoughts which pass into prayer, prayers which pass into love, and love which passes into life with Christ for ever.

HYMN

WORTHY of praise from every mouth,
    of confession from every tongue,
    of worship from every creature,
is your glorious name, O God,
    Father, Son, and Holy Spirit;
for you created the world by the word of your power,
    and in love you most wonderfully redeemed it.
Therefore with angels and archangels,
    and with all the company of heaven,
we proclaim your great and glorious nam
    for ever praising you and saying:
Holy, holy, holy Lord,
God of power and might,
Heaven and earth are full of your glory.
    Hosanna in the highest.

OUR FATHER...

CANTICLE OR PSALM

BIBLE READING

GOD the Father, beyond our highest thought and deepest knowledge, to whom we offer our worship;

God the Son, companion of our human experience, through whom we know and come to the Father;

God the Holy Spirit, helper in our prayers, in whom we have fellowship with the Father through the Son:

grant us that sense of reverence, confidence and community without which our worship cannot be worthy of your sovereignty and your redeeming love.

Open our eyes, O God, to the glory of your wisdom, power and love, that we may worship you with clearer vision, deeper reverence, and greater joy; through Jesus Christ our Lord.

A collect

LORD of all power and might, who art the author and giver of all good things: graft in our hearts the love of thy name, increase in us true religion, nourish us with all goodness, and of thy great mercy keep us in the same; through Jesus Christ our Lord.

SOCIAL JUSTICE

HELP us, O Lord, to understand what your will is in the confusion and unrest of our times. Give us insight to distinguish between the signs of your Spirit demanding change and renewal, and the signs of human greed and lust for power, that we may be your fellow workers in creating an order of society which acknowledges your sovereign love and might.

We pray, Lord, for the victims of injustice in our social order, that voices may be raised on their behalf:

for those who inflict injustice on others, that they may be brought to repentance;

for those who give orders, that they may exercise authority with sensitivity and understanding;

for those who obey orders, that they may do so responsibly and not slavishly;

and for those who work to alleviate the ills of society, that they may know how best to help.

DAILY WORK

LORD Jesus Christ, who hallowed the workshop at Nazareth by your labour, and chose for your disciples men of the fields, the sea and the counting-house: we pray for those who maintain the fabric of the world by their labour. Give them both integrity in their work and charity towards one another, that our common life may do honour to your name.

Almighty God, through whom each act achieves its own perfection: help us to bring our best powers to our work, and to find satisfaction in work well done. And though we cannot fully know the end of what we do, may we in all our dealings keep in mind the image of your love and justice revealed in Jesus Christ our Lord.

THE SPIRIT OF SERVICE

O GOD, our heavenly Father,
whose Son our Lord Jesus Christ
took the form of a servant
   and became the Man for others:
give to us the same spirit of service
   and help us to follow in his steps,

that with love and humility we may give ourselves
to those who need our help.

PARLIAMENT

Eternal Lord God, to whom belong all power and
dominion: we seek the guidance of your Spirit for all
on whom the responsibility of government is laid, and
especially for those who serve in the High Court of
Parliament; that they may have wisdom to order the
affairs of our nation in accordance with your will and for
the glory of your name.

FOR THE DAY

Teach us, our Father, so to live through the hours of
this day that we may come to its end unashamed and
with a quiet mind; through Jesus Christ our Lord.

Give us, O Lord, the humility to acknowledge our
ignorance and to seek your wisdom; and the honesty to
know our weakness and to seek your strength; for Jesus
Christ's sake.

HYMN

THE BLESSING

18

THE KINGDOM OF GOD
('Your kingdom come')

Seek ye first God's kingdom and his righteousness.

Blessed are the poor in spirit, for theirs is the kingdom of heaven.

ETERNAL Lord God, as is your majesty
so is your mercy.
  Open our eyes to your light,
  our hearts to your love,
  and our minds to your truth,
that we may praise you now and always,
  through Jesus Christ our Lord.

HYMN

ALL your creatures praise you, O Lord,
and your servants bless you.
They talk of the glory of your kingdom
  and tell of your might;
they proclaim to their fellows
  how mighty are your deeds,
  how glorious the majesty of your kingdom.
Your kingdom is an everlasting kingdom,
  and your dominion stands for all generations.

O King of men and master of our lives, entering into
glory by your cross, to whom all authority is given both in
heaven and on earth: come, Lord Christ, enter into your

kingdom; subdue the world by the power of your love; be known and adored to all the ends of the earth.

OUR FATHER...

CANTICLE OR PSALM

BIBLE READING

O GOD, to whom we pray for the coming of your kingdom: let this be no vain repetition on our part. Let your kingdom come in us, that all our thoughts, desires and acts may be brought into captivity to Christ. Then take our lives, Lord God, and make them the agents of your kingdom, that through us your will may be done on earth as it is in heaven, to the glory of your name.

O Lord Jesus Christ, made Man for us,
    through whose perfect obedience
the eternal kingdom once took form on earth
    and touched our human life with heavenly glory:
teach us the secret of your humility,
    that we may ourselves enter into your kingdom,
and pray and work for its triumph
    in the hearts of all men.

A collect

ALMIGHTY and merciful God, of whose only gift it cometh that thy faithful people do unto thee true and laudable service: grant, we beseech thee, that we may so faithfully serve thee in this life, that we fail not finally to attain thy heavenly promises; through the merits of Jesus Christ our Lord.

THE SPREAD OF CHRIST'S KINGDOM

ETERNAL God, Father of all mankind, in whom we live and move and have our being: have mercy on the whole human race. Pity their ignorance, their foolishness, their weakness, their sin. Set up an ensign for the nations, O Lord; hasten your kingdom, and bring in everlasting righteousness; for the honour of our Lord and Saviour Jesus Christ.

> Lord, you have consecrated our world
> by sending your Son into the midst of it
> and by making all things new in him.
> We ask you to give us and all your people
> the courage and power we need
> to share fully in his mission to the world
> and to further his kingdom in the lives of men.

WORKERS IN THE CHURCH OVERSEAS

FATHER, we ask you to protect those who cross the world's frontiers as heralds of Christ's kingdom. In times of loneliness support them; in times of disappointment give them patience; in times of frustration strengthen them to persevere; and at all times keep them aware of their dependence on you; through Jesus Christ our Lord.

NON-CHRISTIANS

LORD of all truth, make us as Christians sensitive and humble in our approach to all men. As we learn of their search for truth within other religions, help us also to see your search for them. And grant that what they have learned of you and your love may find its fulfilment in

Christ, through whom we come to the full knowledge of yourself, God blessed for ever.

INTERNATIONAL CO-OPERATION

ALMIGHTY and most merciful Father, whose purpose it is that the kingdoms of this world should become the kingdom of your Son: bestow your blessing on all who are working for righteousness and peace among the peoples, that the day may be hastened when war shall be no more, and your will alone shall govern the nations upon earth; through Jesus Christ our Lord.

Lord, we are grateful that in our day men of many nations meet and work together for peaceful ends. We pray for the United Nations Organisation and its agencies; for the International Red Cross and all similar bodies; that their work may be valued and supported by every nation and bring timely help to the needy places of the earth.

FOR THE DAY

O GOD, set up your kingdom in our hearts and make us your loyal subjects, that we may give our lives to your service and seek to do your will, for the honour of Christ our Lord.

> O Christ our God, in our acts this day,
>> the words we speak,
>> the thoughts we think,
>> the tasks we attempt,
>> the relationships of our common life,
> may your kingdom come, your will be done,
> on earth as in heaven.

HYMN

THE BLESSING

19

THE WILL OF GOD
('Your will be done')

He who doeth the will of God abideth for ever.

Teach me to do the thing that pleaseth thee; for thou art my God.

SET our hearts, O God, at liberty from ourselves, and let it be our meat and drink to do your will; through Jesus Christ our Lord.

HYMN

HEAVENLY Father, we thank you that your will is good and perfect;
    that you will only what is for the true happiness of
      your children;
    and that you have made known this your will for
      mankind in the life and teaching of Jesus Christ.
Have mercy upon us, O Lord, for we have refused your will and gone our own way and found no peace.

Turn us to yourself, and give us the light of your Holy Spirit, that we may see more clearly what our lives ought to be like; and strengthen us to live as children of the light, that we may go on our way pardoned and renewed; through Jesus Christ our Lord.

OUR FATHER...

CANTICLE OR PSALM

BIBLE READING

GOD and Father of us all, whose word proclaims your loving service to mankind and your will that we should be your fellow servants for the kingdom:

we confess with shame our failure to do your will here on earth; our refusal to accept responsibility for our neighbours; our lack of love for those we seek to serve.

Lord, in your mercy forgive what we have been, amend what we are, and direct what we shall be; for Jesus Christ's sake.

Eternal God, the fountain of all wisdom
  and giver of all grace:
so fill us with the light and power
  of your Holy Spirit
that in all our doubts and difficulties
  we may be enabled to know your mind
and to do your will;
  through Jesus Christ our Lord.

A collect

GRANT to us, Lord, we beseech thee, the spirit to think and do always such things as be rightful; that we, who cannot do anything that is good without thee, may by thee be enabled to live according to thy will; through Jesus Christ our Lord.

HEALING OF THE SICK

REMEMBER in mercy, O God our Father, those who are passing through illness, and especially those of whom we are now thinking in our prayers . . . Bless all that is being done for their good, and surround them with your healing love and power, that your will may be done, through Jesus Christ our Lord.

Father, we bring to you in the name of our Lord Jesus Christ those whose lives are broken by ill-health. May your healing Spirit assist all who seek to restore them, that in your goodness they may find wholeness in body, mind and spirit, for the glory of your name.

SOCIAL ORDER

O GOD, whose righteous will it is that all your children should live in peace and equity: forgive the selfishness and stupidity by which men have abused your providence and squandered your gifts. Give wisdom to those who lead the nations and direct our industries; and inspire each of us to share more fairly the produce of the world and to succour those in want; through Jesus Christ our Lord.

God and Father of us all, we pray that in our society we may learn to seek first your kingdom and your righteousness; to care for justice more than for gain, and for fellowship more than for domination; so that in all of us suspicion may give place to trust, and bitterness to goodwill, and we may live together in peace as members one of another.

We bring to you, O God, a world where much is amiss because your will is not done:
a world where men are at war with one another, where the hungry are not fed, where people suffer because of their colour, where the love of many has grown cold.

We confess, O Lord, our own share in all this and ask for your forgiveness.
Give us understanding of your will, fill us with your fear, and lead us in the right way, for your name's sake.

A GENERAL INTERCESSION

WE pray, O Lord, for the life of our world, that guided by your Spirit we may learn
to live together in peace,

to remove from mankind the fear and threat of war,
to share the world's resources,
to secure for every man his fundamental rights,
to provide for all who are in want.
We pray also for your Church as it seeks
to serve the world in the name of Christ,
to share his good news with the nations,
to remind mankind that we do not live by bread alone
and that we are accountable to God for all we do.
God our Father, these are large prayers.
Save them from being empty words on our lips.
Help us to play our part in bringing about the things for
which we pray.

FOR THE DAY

HELP us, O God, to live this day as true followers of
Jesus Christ:
to renounce what is wrong,
to believe what is true,
and to do what is right,
for the glory of his name.

A collect

O ALMIGHTY and most merciful God, of thy bountiful
goodness keep us, we beseech thee, from all things
that may hurt us; that we, being ready both in body and
mind, may cheerfully accomplish those things that thou
wouldest have done: through Jesus Christ our Lord.

HYMN

THE BLESSING

20

OUR DAILY BREAD
('Give us today our daily bread')

Bless the Lord, O my soul, and forget not all his benefits.

Every day will I give thanks unto thee: and praise thy name for ever and ever.

LORD Jesus, the true bread from heaven who came to give life to the world: satisfy the longings of our hearts and fulfil in us your promise that those who come to you shall hunger and thirst no more.

HYMN

LET us thank God for the daily miracle by which our lives are sustained:
for the heat of the sun,
for the good and fruitful earth,
for the changing seasons;
for the labour of men in field and factory,
for the traffic of men on land and sea,
for the service of those in this and other lands by whose work we are fed and clothed and housed;
above all, for him who came to share our lot, to live and labour among men, to pour out his life for the redemption of mankind, and to deliver us from sin and death, Jesus Christ our Lord.

With thankful hearts, O God, we acknowledge your mercy and your love, and we offer you again the service of our lives, through him who taught us to pray:

OUR FATHER...

CANTICLE OR PSALM

BIBLE READING

LORD, you create all things
in your wisdom, love and power;
give us eyes to see the wonder of your works,
   wills that are strong for your service,
and hearts that love you,
   who first loved us.
Lord, forgive our misuse
   of things you have made;
forgive our failure to discern your purpose
   and to share in it.
Make us thankful for all your good gifts
   and faithful in the use of them;
and deepen our trust in your love and care;
   through Jesus Christ our Lord.

A collect

ALMIGHTY God, who seest that we have no power of
ourselves to help ourselves: keep us both outwardly in
our bodies, and inwardly in our souls; that we may be
defended from all adversities which may happen to the
body, and from all evil thoughts which may assault and
hurt the soul; through Jesus Christ our Lord.

THE HUNGRY MILLIONS

O GOD, from whose unfailing bounty we draw our life
and all that we possess: forgive our selfishness and
greed, and our indifference to the needs of others. Touch us
with compassion for the millions in all the world who are
starving and destitute; and as you have given us the know-

ledge which can produce plenty, so give us also the wisdom to bring it within the reach of all; through Jesus Christ our Lord.

We thank you, Lord and Creator of all things, for the blessings of this life and the abundant variety of your gifts; for the food we eat and the pleasure it gives us.

But we know that millions have less than enough while others eat to excess.

Food is wasted while millions starve.

Nature's resources are misused to bring men profit.

Forgive us, Lord, our selfishness, and open our hearts to the needs of the hungry wherever they may be, for the sake of our Lord Jesus Christ.

Heavenly Father, giver of all good things,
    make us more thankful for what we have received;
    make us more content with what we have;
    make us more mindful of people in need;
    and make us more ready to help and serve them in
        whatever way we can,
as servants of Jesus Christ our Lord.

HARVEST

WE thank you, O God our Father, that you so faithfully fulfil your promise to mankind, that seedtime and harvest shall not fail.

We thank you for the fruits of the earth in their season, for the harvest of the seas, and for the food that is brought to us from other lands.

Give us always grateful hearts for these your gifts, and may we who have plenty remember others who have but little, for Jesus Christ's sake.

SEEDTIME

HEAVENLY Father, as you have taught us to pray for our daily bread and to recognise our dependence on your bounty, so we seek your blessing on the sowing of the seed and the labours of your servants; that the earth may yield its full harvest and the needs of all men may be supplied; through Jesus Christ our Lord.

PROPER USE OF NATURAL RESOURCES

ALMIGHTY God, Creator and Lord of all, you have put us in charge of the world and its resources: make us wise in the use of your gifts, that they may serve the welfare and not the destruction of mankind, and that we may be found faithful in stewardship; for the sake of Jesus Christ our Lord.

We rejoice, O Lord, that you have made the earth so rich in natural resources; and we pray that we may learn to use them responsibly:

not wasting them on what we do not need,

not polluting the soil, the air and the sea;

not wantonly destroying the life of animals and plants;

but taking care to hand on to others an earth fit for the life of man, to the honour of your name.

FOR THE DAY

O GOD our Father, we thank you for all the good things of life. Help us to see them, and to number them, and to remember them, that our lives may flow in ceaseless praise; through Jesus Christ our Lord.

May the same mind be in us which was in Christ Jesus; that having his love, his humility, and his obedience always in remembrance, we may consecrate ourselves to the service of others, in his name and for his sake.

HYMN

THE BLESSING

21

FORGIVEN AND FORGIVING

('Forgive us our sins, as we forgive those who sin against us')

*Be kind to one another, tenderhearted, forgiving one another,
as God in Christ forgave you.*

*Make me a clean heart, O God; and renew a right spirit
within me.*

GRANT, we beseech thee, merciful Lord, to thy faithful
people pardon and peace; that they may be cleansed
from all their sins, and serve thee with a quiet mind;
through Jesus Christ our Lord.

HYMN

ALMIGHTY God, our heavenly Father,
we have sinned against you and against our fellow
men,
in thought and word and deed,
in the evil we have done
and in the good we have not done,
through ignorance, through weakness,
through our own deliberate fault.
We are truly sorry and repent of all our sins.
For the sake of your Son Jesus Christ,
who died for us,
forgive us all that is past;
and grant that we may serve you in newness of life;
to the glory of your name.

OUR FATHER...

CANTICLE OR PSALM

BIBLE READING

ETERNAL Father, you have never ceased to call us your children, even though we have so often resisted your will and gone our own ways. We pray that out of your full store of grace we sinners may once again receive pardon, an end to guilt and anxiety, a new beginning to endeavour, and a fresh vision of your purpose for our lives; through Jesus Christ our Lord.

Heavenly Father, you have taught us by your Son
    that if we do not forgive others
    we cannot receive your forgiveness:
make us merciful in our dealings with those who do us
        wrong,
    as we recall how mercifully you have dealt with us;
that forgiven much, we may forgive much,
    for the sake of him who died that we might be
        forgiven,
    our Saviour Jesus Christ.

Father, help us who have been forgiven to be tender and compassionate towards those who are overtaken by temptation, considering how we ourselves have fallen in times past, and may yet fall again; and may we neither presume upon your forgiveness by living carelessly, nor doubt it and be weighed down by guilt; for Jesus Christ's sake.

RECONCILIATION

O LORD Jesus Christ, Prince of peace, break down the barriers which separate men from each other and from God.

Teach Christians to love one another across the walls of colour, class and creed.

Forgive the excuses we make for our own prejudices; and lead us captive in your cause of peace on earth, goodwill to men, for your name's sake.

Lord Christ, who by your cross and passion
    reconciled the world to God
and broke down the barriers of race and colour
    which divide men and nations:
make us and all your people
    instruments of reconciliation in the life of our world,
that we may inherit the blessing
    which you promised to the peacemakers.

THOSE IN TROUBLE

CHRIST our Lord, friend of outcasts and sinners, grant to all offenders against the law the gift of repentance and the knowledge of your forgiveness; and so renew a right spirit within them that they may find true joy and freedom in your service.

Our heavenly Father, we commend to your mercy those for whom life does not spell freedom:
    prisoners of conscience,
    the homeless and the handicapped,
    the sick in body and mind,
    the elderly who are confined to their homes,
    those who are enslaved by their passions,
    and those who are addicted to drugs.
Grant that, whatever their outward circumstances, they may find inward freedom, through him who proclaimed release to captives, Jesus Christ our Saviour.

WAR VICTIMS

FATHER of mercies, whose Son here on earth
ministered to those in need:
remember for good all who suffer through war
　　by loss of home or health,
　　by loss of friends and loved ones,
　　by loss of security and freedom,
　　by loss of faith and hope.
Look upon our world, still torn apart by violence,
　　and prosper the work of all who are striving for peace;
through Jesus Christ our Lord.

Have mercy, O God, on those who are victims of man's
inhumanity to man:
　　defenceless people in hideous war zones;
　　families robbed of those they love;
　　prisoners of war, ill-treated and tortured;
　　old people and children dying of starvation;
　　and those who still bear the scars of former wars.
Deepen our pity, O Lord, into creative prayer which
will inspire us to positive action, for the sake of our
Saviour Jesus Christ.

A GENERAL INTERCESSION

ETERNAL God, in whose will is our peace, we commend
to your mercy the needs of all the world:
　　where there is hatred, give love;
　　where there is injury, pardon;
　　where there is doubt, faith;
　　where there is despair, hope;
　　where there is darkness, light;
　　where there is sadness, joy;
for the sake of Jesus Christ our Lord.

FOR THE DAY

O GOD, forgive us the sins which have so laid hold upon us that we no longer confess them to be sins. May your Spirit enlighten us, cleanse us and strengthen us, and enable us this day to live to your glory.

A collect

O LORD, we beseech thee, absolve thy people from their offences; that through thy bountiful goodness we may all be delivered from the bands of those sins, which by our frailty we have committed. Grant this, O heavenly Father, for Jesus Christ's sake, our blessed Lord and Saviour.

HYMN

THE BLESSING

22

KEPT BY THE POWER OF GOD
('Deliver us from evil')

They that wait upon the Lord shall renew their strength.

God is our refuge and strength, a very present help in trouble.

Comfort, O Lord, the soul of thy servant; for unto thee do I lift up my soul.

Look upon us with your mercy, O God; that we who now wait upon you in weakness may be made strong through the grace of our Lord Jesus Christ.

HYMN

Father, we confess that although our voices join the praises of your people, our actions have not been in tune with our words.

We have failed in our duty to you and to our neighbour, yielding to temptation, adding to evil, and neglecting many opportunities of doing good.

Have mercy upon us, O Lord. Help us, each one, to lay at your feet now the burden of our guilt. Accept us, and set us free.

May we find, in this act of worship, inspiration and strength to rejoin the battle against the powers of darkness in ourselves and in the world; through Jesus Christ our Lord.

OUR FATHER...

CANTICLE OR PSALM

BIBLE READING

HOLY Spirit of God, inspirer of all that is good and beautiful and true: come into our hearts and fill them with your abundant life. Help us to hate all sin and to fight against it with unfaltering courage and resolve; and because we are weak and cannot prevail without your help, strengthen us and give us the victory through our Lord Jesus Christ.

> Open our minds, O Lord,
>   to see ourselves as you see us,
> and deliver us from all blindness of heart,
>   from all hypocrisy and pretence.
> Save us from pride and self-will,
>   from jealousy and uncharitableness,
>   from sloth and moral weakness,
> and arm us with your strength
>   in face of all temptation and adversity.

A collect

O GOD, who knowest us to be set in the midst of so many and great dangers, that by reason of the frailty of our nature we cannot always stand upright: grant to us such strength and protection as may support us in all dangers, and carry us through all temptations; through Jesus Christ our Lord.

THOSE IN NEED

HEAVENLY Father, we remember before you all children in need: the orphaned, the homeless, the unwanted; the children of broken homes, and those who suffer from bodily defect or disease. Protect them from all evil, and make us vigilant to guard them and care for them in the name of our Saviour Jesus Christ.

Lord Jesus Christ, you know the perils and hazards of human life: hear us as we remember in your presence
those whose work is dangerous,
those who risk their lives to rescue others,
those who are victims of violence,
those who suffer from incurable disease.
We commend them in your name, O Christ, to God's infinite love and merciful care.

Christ our Saviour, the strength of the weak, the friend of all in need: guard and deliver the tempted; reveal your grace to the fallen; maintain the faith of those who are persecuted for righteousness' sake; and console with your presence all who are disappointed, lonely, or in despair; for your tender mercy's sake.

THE SPIRITUAL WAR

LORD Christ, who as the Son of Man knew the weakness of our nature and the power of temptation and yet overcame in the fight: so breathe into our hearts the strength of your Spirit that we may conquer all that wars against the soul, and may be kept your faithful soldiers and servants to the end.

Lord God, you have called us by your grace to be soldiers of Christ and to fight manfully under his banner: enable us at all times to contend for justice, truth and goodness without fear or favour, and relentlessly to oppose evil wherever it is found, and whatever form it takes, for the honour of our Lord Jesus Christ.

Strengthen us, O God, for the warfare of the Spirit, that we may stand fast in the day of testing, and in all things may prove more than conquerors through him who loves us, Jesus Christ our Lord.

A GENERAL PETITION

O GOD, almighty and merciful, deliver us and all men from the power of sin:

from the evil which infects the world we live in;

from the fears and faithlessness of our own hearts;

from pride and all forms of self-deception;

from self-concern, and indifference to the needs of others;

from the blindness which sees no difference between good and evil;

from the sloth which allows evil to pass for good.

Lift us above our failures, and let your forgiveness restore us and your power remake us in Jesus Christ our Lord.

FOR THE DAY

D ELIVER us, Lord, from every evil,
and grant us peace in our day.
In your mercy keep us free from sin
and protect us from all anxiety,
as we wait in joyful hope
for the coming of our Saviour Jesus Christ.

A collect

L ORD, we beseech thee, grant thy people grace to withstand the temptations of the world, the flesh, and the devil, and with pure hearts and minds to follow thee the only God; through Jesus Christ our Lord.

HYMN

THE BLESSING

23

THE PRESENCE OF GOD

Be still, and know that I am God.

Lo, I am with you always, even unto the end.

Hold thee still in the Lord: and abide patiently upon him.

ALMIGHTY God and Father, help us to be still in your presence, that we may know ourselves to be your people, and you to be our God; through Jesus Christ our Lord.

HYMN

LORD, we come to you in the assurance that you are present with us now.

We do not have to seek your presence.

We are daily living in your presence.

Make us aware of it.

Make it real to us.

And help us in these moments of prayer to know that we are speaking to one who is near and not far off, whose love is all around us and who knows our every need.

So may we be relaxed in your presence and our hearts be at peace.

We ask it through our Saviour Jesus Christ, and in his name we pray:

OUR FATHER...

CANTICLE OR PSALM

BIBLE READING

ALMIGHTY God, in whose presence is the fullness of joy, and whose power is made perfect in our weakness: enable us so to dwell in your presence that we may have your peace in our hearts; and so to rest on your strength that we may have victory over evil; through Jesus Christ our Lord.

> Lord Jesus Christ, you have promised
>   to be with us always, to the end of time:
> teach us to live as ever in your presence,
>   that we may be kept from sinning,
>   and be free from all needless anxiety,
>   and be guided in the way that we should go,
> to the glory of God the Father.

A collect

O ALMIGHTY God, who alone canst order the unruly wills and affections of sinful men: grant unto thy people, that they may love the thing which thou commandest, and desire that which thou dost promise; that so, among the sundry and manifold changes of the world, our hearts may surely there be fixed where true joys are to be found; through Jesus Christ our Lord.

THE CHURCH IN OUR LAND

BESTOW your blessing, O Lord our God, upon your Church in our land, that through its witness increasing numbers may hear your word, receive it, and live by it.

May its power be seen more and more in the lives of those who believe.

So prosper your work among us, O God, in this our generation, that the doubter may be convinced, the wavering established, the sinful converted, and the faithful multiplied, for the glory of our Lord Jesus Christ.

Be present in your power, O Lord,
    with the mission of your Church in this land.
Give your people grace to bear their witness
    with courage and zeal,
and to commend the gospel of Christ
    both by the sincerity of their faith
    and by the consistency of their lives,
for the glory of your name.

O God, whose matchless power is ever new and ever young: pour out your Spirit on us and on all our fellow Christians; that with increased faith, vision and obedience we may the more joyfully testify to your new creation in Christ, and more selflessly serve your new order amid the old.

THE LONELY

O GOD of love, present in all places and at all times, pour your Spirit of healing and comfort on every lonely heart. Have pity on those who are bereft of human love, and on those to whom love has never come. Be to them a strong consolation, an ever-present help; and in the end give them fullness of joy, for the sake of Jesus Christ our Lord.

O Lord our God, you have said,
    'I will never leave you nor forsake you':
grant that all who pass their days in loneliness
    may be strong and of good courage,
    knowing that you are with them;
and make us ready to visit and cheer them
    in their need,
for the sake of Jesus Christ our Lord.

IN TIMES OF ANXIETY

HAVE mercy upon us, our Father, in those hours when the world seems empty of your presence, and no word comes to reassure our hearts; that in the darkness we may wait patiently for the light, and in the silence listen for your voice, and in all things trust your promises in Jesus Christ our Lord.

FOR THE DAY

TEACH us, O God, to walk trustfully today in your presence; that your voice may encourage us, your arm defend us, and your love surround us; through Jesus Christ our Lord.

God our Father, we pray that your presence may bless us, guard us and strengthen us all through this day, that our lives may be of service to others and bring glory to your name.

HYMN

THE BLESSING

24

THE WORD OF GOD

Heaven and earth shall pass away, but my words shall not pass away.

Blessed are they that hear the word of God, and keep it.

LORD, you spoke by the prophets,
and you have spoken to us in your Son:
guide our minds by your Spirit,
　　that we may understand your word.
May it prove in us and in the world
　　a word of life and power.

HYMN

WE give thanks, O God, for the wonder of your dealings with men, from the beginning until now:
for your creative word, by which the heavens and the earth were made;
for making man in your own image, able to hear and answer your call;
for the written word, which has been a lamp to our feet, and still shines upon our way;
for the mystery of the word made flesh in the coming of our Lord Jesus Christ;
for the preservation of your true and living word in the Church;
for your word to us in these days, calling us to repentance and assuring us of pardon;
we thank you, O Lord, and praise your name.

OUR FATHER...

CANTICLE OR PSALM

BIBLE READING

WRITE upon our hearts, O Lord God, the lessons of your holy word, and grant that we may be doers of that word and not hearers only; through Jesus Christ our Lord.

Enable us, our God and Father,
   to respond to the grace of your word
with humility of heart and mind
   and in the spirit of loving obedience;
that our wills may be brought into submission
   to your perfect will,
and our lives be conformed more and more
   to the image of your Son Jesus Christ.

Heavenly Father, you have given us the scriptures
   that through them we may have eternal life
   by believing in your Son:
help us so to receive your word into our hearts
   that we may find light for our way,
   strength in our weakness,
   and comfort in our distress.

A collect

BLESSED Lord, who hast caused all holy scriptures to be written for our learning: grant that we may in such wise hear them, read, mark, learn, and inwardly digest them; that by patience, and comfort of thy holy word, we may embrace, and ever hold fast, the blessed hope of everlasting life, which thou hast given us in our Saviour Jesus Christ.

MINISTERS OF THE WORD

Pour out your Holy Spirit, O Lord, on all whom you have called to serve your Church as pastors and teachers.

Give them wise and understanding hearts;
fill them with a true love for your people;
make them holy and keep them humble;
that they may serve you faithfully and advance the kingdom of our Lord Jesus Christ.

Strengthen by your grace, O Lord God,
    all ministers of the gospel,
that they may be leaders of men
    in honesty of thought,
    simplicity of life,
    and sincerity of faith,
and so be faithful shepherds of Christ's flock,
    for the glory of his name.

O God, may the same mind be in all ministers of your Church that was in Christ Jesus:
    his self-forgetting humility,
    his love for common people,
    his compassion for the fallen,
    his forbearance with the mistaken,
    his patience with the slow;
and in all their words and work make them continually sensitive to your guidance and ready for your will.

BROADCASTERS AND JOURNALISTS

Almighty God, whose truth has been declared of old by the voice of prophets and evangelists: direct the minds of those who speak in our day where many listen and write what many read; that they may do their part in making the heart of our people wise, their mind sound, and their will righteous; to the honour of your name.

Father, we thank you that you have spoken to us through the words of scripture, and chiefly through him who is the living Word of God.

We pray for all who, by what they say and write, influence the lives of others; for those whose daily task is in the use of words.

We ask for them reverence for the truth, sensitiveness to human need, and a true concern for the welfare of the community.

DISCIPLESHIP

O GOD, you have called us to the life of discipleship: make us better disciples.

You have taught us something of your truth: teach us still more.

Give us at all times openness of mind and humility of heart, that we may learn your will and follow more closely in the steps of Christ our Lord.

Lord Jesus Christ, as you have called us to be your disciples, so make us ready to learn all that you wish to teach us. May our eyes never be blind to your truth, nor our ears deaf to your call, but in all the tasks of life may we seek your will and serve your kingdom.

FOR THE DAY

THE things, good Lord, that your servants pray for, give us grace also to work for; and in the purpose of your love both answer our prayers and prosper our endeavours; for Jesus Christ our Saviour's sake.

Father, give to us, and to all your people,
  in times of anxiety, serenity;
  in times of hardship, courage;
  in times of uncertainty, patience;
  and at all times a quiet trust in your wisdom and love,
through Jesus Christ our Lord.

HYMN

THE BLESSING

25

WALK IN THE LIGHT

I am the light of the world. He that followeth me shall not walk in darkness, but shall have the light of life.

God is light, and in him is no darkness at all.

O GOD, who commanded the light to shine out of darkness: shine in our hearts, to give the light of the knowledge of your glory in the face of Jesus Christ.

HYMN

GOD is light, and in him there is no darkness at all. If we claim to be sharing in his life while we walk in the dark, our words and our lives are a lie.

But if we walk in the light, as he himself is in the light, then we share a common life and we are being cleansed from sin by the blood of Jesus.

Lord, you are light and you give us light; but we are often in the darkness, and the world is in the darkness, because we do not look to your light and trust in you.

We are in the darkness, and the world is in the darkness, because we live in our own way and do not love each other as you love us.

Lord, forgive us, and dispel our darkness with your light, through Jesus Christ who is the light of the world.

OUR FATHER...

CANTICLE OR PSALM

BIBLE READING

WE give thanks, O God our Father, that you have awakened us again to praise your goodness and to seek your grace. Make us children of the light and of the day, that our lives may reflect your glory and we may shine as lights in the world; through Jesus Christ our Lord.

Heavenly Father, by whose grace we have been called
out of darkness into your marvellous light;
open our eyes to see your purpose for our lives;
and give us such obedience in the things we know
that fresh light may shine upon our way,
and we may grow daily in the knowledge of your
will.

A collect

ALMIGHTY God, who showest to them that be in error the light of thy truth, to the intent that they may return into the way of righteousness: grant unto all them that are admitted into the fellowship of Christ's religion, that they may eschew those things that are contrary to their profession, and follow all such things as are agreeable to the same; through our Lord Jesus Christ.

EDUCATION

GUIDE, O Lord our God, the minds of those who direct the work of education, and prosper with your blessing the schools and colleges of this land; that our boys and girls and young people may be equipped with faith and knowledge for the journey of life, and be strong in spirit to serve their generation by your will; through Jesus Christ our Lord.

Send your blessing, O Lord,
upon the work of all universities and colleges.

Enlighten by your Spirit
    those who teach and those who learn,
and lead them further on in their quest
    for truth and knowledge,
    for faith and freedom,
that the life of mankind may be enriched by their studies;
    through Jesus Christ our Lord.

Lord Jesus Christ, in whom are hidden all the treasures of wisdom and knowledge: we pray for the students of every nation. Guide them by your Spirit into all truth; and make them to know that the fear of the Lord is the beginning of wisdom, that as they consecrate their lives to your service, they may find in you the way, the truth and the life.

THOSE WHO WORK AT NIGHT

BLESS, O Lord, those who by night watch over our lives and homes, and guard those who carry on the unresting commerce of the world by land and sea and air. Give them rest and refreshment, and make us thankful for their service; through Jesus Christ our Lord.

Let your presence, O God, refresh and strengthen those who have watched through the night on behalf of others, in sickroom and in hospital, and give them your peace; through Jesus Christ our Lord.

THE BLIND

LORD Christ, when you gave sight to the blind in your ministry on earth you spoke about a greater power of inward sight: we pray that those who cannot see the world about them may perceive the things of eternal worth, and receive from those near to them a friendship and care which will help them to overcome their handicap and will be a light to their path.

IN TIME OF DOUBT

LORD, when it is dark and we cannot feel your presence, and nothing seems real any more, and we are tempted to give up trying, help us to remember that you are never really absent and to trust you still; so may we rest in your love, and know that underneath are the everlasting arms.

FOR THE DAY

HEAVENLY Father, we give you hearty thanks for the light of this new day. May we so spend its hours in the perfect freedom of your service, that when evening comes we may again give you thanks; through Jesus Christ our Lord.

God our Father, direct and control us in every part of our life:

our tongues, that we speak no false or angry words;
our actions, that we may do nothing to shame ourselves or hurt others;
our minds, that we may think no evil or bitter thoughts;
our hearts, that they may be set only on pleasing you;
through Jesus Christ our Lord.

HYMN

THE BLESSING

26

THE GOOD SHEPHERD

*He is the Lord our God; and we are the people of his pasture,
and the sheep of his hand.*

*I am the good shepherd; the good shepherd layeth down his
life for the sheep.*

O GOD our Shepherd, bring us in this time of worship
to the green pastures and lead us beside the still waters,
that in your presence we may find refreshment, and our
hearts may be at rest.

HYMN

ALMIGHTY and most merciful Father, we have erred and
strayed from your ways like lost sheep.
We have followed too much the devices and desires of
our own hearts.
We have left undone those things which we ought to
have done, and we have done those things which we ought
not to have done, and there is no health in us.
Have mercy upon us, O Lord.
Pardon and deliver us from all our sins.
Confirm and strengthen us in all goodness;
and bring us to everlasting life;
through Jesus Christ our Lord.

OUR FATHER...

CANTICLE OR PSALM

BIBLE READING

GOOD Shepherd, who laid down your life for the sheep: we commit our lives to your guidance and protection, that we may not fear the dangers of the way, but follow where you lead, and journey on in your strength with trustful hearts.

Lord Jesus, the good shepherd of the sheep,
    have compassion on those who have wandered from
      you;
    feed those who are hungry;
    cause the weary to lie down in your pastures;
    bind up those who are broken in heart;
    and lead us all, O Lord, in the paths of righteousness,
      for your name's sake.

A collect

O GOD, whose never-failing providence ordereth all things both in heaven and earth: we humbly beseech thee to put away from us all hurtful things, and to give us those things which be profitable for us; through Jesus Christ our Lord.

THOSE IN NEED

COMFORT, most gracious Father, all who are cast down and fearful of heart amid the darkness and sorrow of the world; and so console and strengthen them by your Holy Spirit that they may go on their way with faith renewed and hope rekindled; through Jesus Christ our Lord.

For those in need, O Lord, we make our prayer:
    the sick in mind or in body,
    the blind and the deaf,
    the fatherless and the widow,
    the sorrowing, the anxious, and the perplexed.

Give them courage, patience, and peace of heart,
and do for them whatever is for their good,
for Jesus Christ's sake.

Have mercy, O God, on any who are lonely or neglected;
and comfort all for whom life is darkened through the loss
of someone greatly loved. Be with them in sorrow and in
loneliness, and give them faith to look beyond their
troubles to you, their heavenly Father and their unchanging
friend.

MENTAL HEALTH

LORD Jesus Christ, you healed many who were mentally
ill, and in your name we pray for a deeper understanding of those whose minds are disturbed. Give knowledge
and skill to those who treat them, patience and kindness to
those who nurse them; and draw together in a closer
fellowship of healing all who are working to further your
will by making men whole.

Lord, we pray for the mentally ill,
    for all who are of a disturbed and troubled mind.
Be to them light in their darkness,
    their refuge and strength in time of fear.
Give special skills and tender hearts
    to all who care for them,
and show them how best to assist your work of healing,
    through Jesus Christ our Lord.

THE ABSENT

LORD of all time and space,
    with whom there is neither distance nor absence,
    and no separation from your love:
we commend to your care our absent friends.

Cheer their spirits,
  lighten their burdens,
  prosper their labours;
and keep them rejoicing in hope, now and at all times,
  for your love's sake.

FOR THE DAY

Good Shepherd, we commit ourselves and all those we
love to your care this day, praying that you will guard
us from every danger and guide us in the right way, for
your name's sake.

A collect

O LORD our heavenly Father, almighty and everlasting
God, who hast safely brought us to the beginning of
this day: defend us in the same with thy mighty power;
and grant that this day we fall into no sin, neither run into
any kind of danger; but that all our doings may be ordered
by thy governance, to do always that is righteous in thy
sight; through Jesus Christ our Lord.

HYMN

THE BLESSING

27

LOVE ONE ANOTHER

This is my commandment, that ye love one another, as I have loved you.

Be ye followers of God, and walk in love, even as Christ loved us, and gave himself for us.

LET the fire of your love, O God, so cleanse and possess us now, that with pure hearts and minds we may offer you our worship and glorify your name, through Jesus Christ our Lord.

HYMN

LORD God our Father, you loved us
before we could love you,
and you gave your Son Jesus Christ
to show us the greatness of your love.
We confess that we have not loved one another
with the love that we see in Christ.
Father, forgive us for being so concerned about ourselves,
for thinking so little about others,
for doing so much less than we should in the cause of
your kingdom.
Fill our lives with the love that finds
no service too costly,
no rejection too hard to bear,
that we may be ready to give all for your sake,
and for the sake of others,
even as Christ in his love
gave all for us.

OUR FATHER...

CANTICLE OR PSALM

BIBLE READING

LORD Jesus, you have taught us that love is the fulfilling
of the law.

Teach us now what love really is,

how much it costs,

how deep it digs into our selfish lives.

Then give us the courage and the generosity to accept
what this means for today and tomorrow and for the whole
course of our lives.

Son of Man, our brother, you have taught us that
whatever we do to the least of your brethren we do to you:
give us grace always to be ready to serve our fellows, and to
see you in all who are poor and needy, for your love's sake.

A collect

O LORD, who hast taught us that all our doings without
charity are nothing worth: send thy Holy Spirit, and
pour into our hearts that most excellent gift of charity, the
very bond of peace and of all virtues, without which
whosoever liveth is counted dead before thee; grant this
for thine only Son Jesus Christ's sake.

PARENTS, TEACHERS AND CHILDREN

O GOD our Father, we ask you to bless all children, and
to give to those who have the care of them wisdom,
patience, and love; so that the homes in which they grow
up may be to them an image of your kingdom, and the
care of their parents a likeness of your love.

Almighty Father, the source of all wisdom and grace, enlighten the minds of those who devote themselves to the teaching of the young. Give them understanding of their task, and love for those they serve; and help them both in their lives and by their teaching to set forward the cause of true religion and sound learning; through Jesus Christ our Lord.

God of all the families of men, we commend to you the homes of our nation.

Preserve to us the sanctities of family life.

Unite us in our homes in true affection one to another.

And give wisdom to all Christian parents and teachers, that they may bring up their children in true faith and in obedience to your word.

THE CHURCH'S SERVICE OF HUMANITY

ETERNAL God and Father, whose Son Jesus Christ came not to be served but to serve,
and to give his life a ransom for many:
fill your whole Church throughout the world
with his spirit of self-sacrifice;
that in its service of mankind
it may be the agent of your love,
and in meeting human need
may make your glory known.

Christ our Saviour, when you beheld the people you were moved with compassion towards them and healed the sick, fed the hungry, and raised the fallen. Pour out upon your Church the same spirit of love. Go forth with all who minister in your name to relieve suffering; and grant that by their service the hearts of men may be drawn to you.

OUR USE OF FREEDOM

ALMIGHTY God, we thank you for the liberties which this country enjoys, and for those who have worked and fought and suffered to secure them:

for freedom from war and want;
for freedom of thought, conscience and speech;
and for freedom of worship.

Give us grace to defend these liberties and to use them responsibly in your service; through Jesus Christ our Lord.

We thank you, our Father, that through Jesus Christ you have set us free from slavery to the ways of the world, from the tyranny of sin and the terror of death. Help us to recognise you as our deliverer and to put our lives fully at your disposal; that serving one another in love we may acknowledge ourselves to be, above all, servants of Christ our Lord.

FOR THE DAY

O GOD, whose compassions fail not, give us grace so to recognise and receive your mercies that we may fashion our own lives after the pattern of your love, and learn to give as freely as we have received.

Lord, help us to understand
what has been done for our redemption,
so that Christ may live in our hearts by faith,
and be proclaimed in our lives by love.

HYMN

THE BLESSING

28

LORD OF THE NATIONS

The Lord has bared his holy arm before the eyes of all the nations; and all the ends of the earth shall see the salvation of our God.

O send out thy light and thy truth that they may lead me: and bring me unto thy holy hill and to thy dwelling.

O GOD and Father of all, whom the whole heavens adore:
let the whole earth also worship you,
all kingdoms obey you,
all tongues confess and bless you,
and the sons of men love and serve you in peace.

HYMN

WE thank you, O Lord, for revealing yourself to man, and for all who have been your messengers in the world:
for the first apostles of Christ, sent out to preach the gospel to every nation;
for those who brought the good news to our own land;
for all who in ages of darkness shone as lights in the world;
for all your followers in every age who have given their lives for the faith;
for those in our own day who have gone to the ends of the earth as heralds of your love;
for the innumerable company who now praise you out of every race and nation.

With these and with your whole Church we worship you and magnify your holy name.

OUR FATHER...

CANTICLE OR PSALM

BIBLE READING

HEAVENLY Father, we pray for your blessing upon us and upon your Church throughout the world, that the cross of Jesus may be lifted high before the nations, and all men everywhere may come to own him as their Saviour and their King.

Eternal God, Lord of the nations, whose love is without limit and without end: enlarge our vision of your redeeming purpose for the world, and help us to co-operate with you in fulfilling your design to bring all men into your family through Jesus Christ, to whom be glory for ever and ever.

A collect

GRANT, O Lord, we beseech thee, that the course of this world may be so peaceably ordered by thy governance, that thy Church may joyfully serve thee in all godly quietness; through Jesus Christ our Lord.

A BETTER WORLD

LORD, give to the nations wisdom to understand the things that belong to their peace, and the will to reject the things that make for war. And we pray that, realising our common humanity, we may live together as a family and make the world a home, bearing one another's burdens, ministering to one another's needs, and obeying your laws in righteousness, as children of one God and Father in Jesus Christ our Lord.

Almighty God, by the power of whose love
    we can live as members of one human family:
give wisdom, right judgment, and an understanding of
    the times
    to all who work to make the world a better place;
and grant that, striving together in unity of purpose
    and constancy of faith,
they may build an order of righteousness and peace;
    through Jesus Christ our Lord.

Father, we pray for all those who are seeking for the
nations of the world a way by which order and freedom
may be maintained, and the differences of peoples be justly
resolved. Establish their purpose on strong foundations,
and guide and prosper their work by your Holy Spirit;
for the sake of Jesus Christ our Lord.

THE CHURCH'S MISSION

WE pray, O God, for your Church throughout the
world, that Christians may respond wholeheartedly
to your love by committing themselves to the service of
your kingdom, with faith strengthened by a living experience of Christ's presence, and with freedom and
courage to follow where Christ leads, for the honour of his
name.

Almighty God, you have called your Church
    to share in your mission to the whole world:
give to us and to all your people
    such belief in the gospel
    and such faithfulness in service
that the life of mankind may be renewed
    in the knowledge and love of your Son,
    Jesus Christ our Lord.

PEOPLE OF OTHER RELIGIONS

D RAW us closer, our Father, to those among our neighbours who practise a religion different from our own.
Help us not to trample on what they hold sacred, but to
respect their convictions, to learn from them insights we
have neglected or forgotten, and to share with them the
light of truth we have received through Jesus Christ.

> Eternal God, Father of all mankind,
>   you have shown yourself to the world in many ways,
> and have never left yourself without witness
>   in the lives of men:
> hear our prayer for people
>   whose faith and customs differ from ours.
> Make us ready to learn from them,
>   and also eager to share with them
> the riches of your truth, which you have given us
>   in Jesus Christ our Lord.

FOR THE DAY

G UIDE us, O Lord, in all we think and say and do this
day, and bless us with your peace; for the sake of
Jesus Christ our Lord.

> Lord Jesus, our leader, we give ourselves to you
> for the cause of your glorious kingdom:
>   for joy or for sorrow,
>   for success or for failure,
>   for life or for death,
> now and for evermore.

HYMN

THE BLESSING

29

IN THE STRENGTH OF GOD

In the world you shall have tribulation; but be of good cheer, I have overcome the world.

The Lord is the strength of my life: of whom then shall I be afraid?

ETERNAL God and Father, in whose presence we find rest and peace: as we come to you now may we be cleansed and strengthened by your Spirit, and serve you with a quiet mind.

HYMN

ALMIGHTY God, we wait on you now
to renew our strength.
You can do for us more than we ask or think;
your grace is sufficient for us,
your strength is made perfect in our weakness.

Give us strength of body to do your work well
and not to be a burden to others.
Give us strength of mind to know what is true
and to hold it fast.
Give us strength of heart to love you,
and to love one another in you.

Lord God, strong and mighty,
the refuge of all who put their trust in you,
in your strength may we find peace,
through Jesus Christ our Lord.

OUR FATHER...

CANTICLE OR PSALM

BIBLE READING

GIVE us grace, O God, to follow you in the darkness as in the light; that for your sake we may face difficulty and adversity, and in your strength be more than conquerors; through Jesus Christ our Lord.

O Lord our God, give us courage:
> courage to make experiments, and not to be afraid of making mistakes;
> courage to get up when we are down and to go forward again;
> courage to persevere in the service of your kingdom and never to lose heart;

for the honour of our Lord Jesus Christ.

A collect

O GOD, the strength of all them that put their trust in thee, mercifully accept our prayers; and because through the weakness of our mortal nature we can do no good thing without thee, grant us the help of thy grace, that in keeping of thy commandments we may please thee, both in will and deed; through Jesus Christ our Lord.

RULERS AND STATESMEN

GRANT, O Lord, to all the leaders of men the wisdom to seek what is right, and the will to do it. May every advance in knowledge, science and technology be directed to good ends, and may godliness among men lead to peace among nations; through Jesus Christ our Lord.

O God, give to the rulers of this land,
    and to all the leaders of the nations,
the vision to look beyond racial ambitions
    and national boundaries;
that in obedience to your laws,
    and with concern for the needs of others,
they may bring their gifts and treasures
    into the common service of your kingdom,
and so promote the unity of all mankind,
    to the glory of your name.

THE PERSECUTED

O GOD, the refuge and strength of your people
    in every time of need:
we pray for all who are persecuted
    for their religious faith
    or their political opinions.
In your mercy give them
    strength to endure their afflictions,
    grace to forgive their persecutors,
    and courage to maintain their testimony
until the day of their deliverance;
    through Jesus Christ our Lord.

Lord Christ, you have shown us that he who witnesses for you must be ready to take up his cross: give strength, hope and endurance to all who suffer for your sake, and keep them in your peace because they trust in you, their crucified and risen Lord.

IN OLD AGE

LORD Jesus Christ, who heard the prayer of your disciples to abide with them when it was towards evening and the day was far spent: abide with your aged servants in the evening of their life and give them the comfort of your presence; and when they shall pass through the valley of the shadow of death, be with them to the end.

THE SICK

LORD Christ our Saviour, in the days of your flesh the sick were brought to you for healing:
hear us as we now bring to you in our prayers
    those who are ill, in body or in mind.
May your presence be with them
    to relieve suffering and distress
    and to restore them to fullness of health,
for your great love's sake.

FOR THE DAY

TEACH us, O God, to begin our works with faith, to go on with obedience, and to finish them in love; and then to wait patiently in hope, knowing that your promises can never fail; through Jesus Christ our Lord.

Sir Francis Drake's prayer

O LORD God, when thou givest to thy servants to endeavour any great matter, grant us to know that it is not the beginning but the continuing of the same unto the end, until it be thoroughly finished, which yieldeth the true glory; through him who for the finishing of thy work laid down his life, even our Redeemer Jesus Christ.

HYMN

THE BLESSING

30

THE HOPE OF GLORY

This is life eternal, that they may know thee, and Jesus Christ whom thou hast sent.

He that sitteth upon the throne saith, Behold, I make all things new.

ALMIGHTY God, from whose love neither death nor life can separate us: with the whole company of the redeemed in heaven and on earth we praise and magnify your glorious name, Father, Son, and Holy Spirit, one God, blessed for ever.

HYMN

BLESSED be the God and Father
of our Lord Jesus Christ!
By his great mercy we have been born anew
to a living hope
through the resurrection of Jesus Christ
from the dead,
and to an inheritance which is imperishable,
undefiled and unfading,
reserved in heaven
for all who put their faith in God.

We praise you, O God our Father, for the hope of our calling:

for the victory of our Lord Jesus Christ, who has broken the power of death and brought life and immortality to light through the gospel;

for the eternal home which he has gone to prepare for us

and for his promise to come again and receive us to himself;

for the great multitude which no man can number, out of every nation, who stand before the throne, and with whom in our Lord we for evermore are one.

OUR FATHER...

CANTICLE OR PSALM

BIBLE READING

ETERNAL Father, of whom the whole family in heaven and on earth is named, unite us in our worship with all who in other places are lifting up their hearts in prayer; that your whole Church throughout the world, with the Church in heaven, may offer up one sacrifice of thanksgiving, to the praise and honour of your name.

> O Lord, the first and the last,
>   the beginning and the end:
> you who were with us at our birth,
>   be with us through our life;
> you who are with us through our life,
>   be with us at our death;
> and because your mercy will not leave us then,
>   grant that we die not,
>   but rise to the life everlasting.

A collect

O GOD, the protector of all that trust in thee, without whom nothing is strong, nothing is holy: increase and multiply upon us thy mercy; that thou being our ruler and guide, we may so pass through things temporal, that we finally lose not the things eternal. Grant this, O heavenly Father, for Jesus Christ's sake our Lord.

THE COMMUNION OF SAINTS

ETERNAL God, before whose face the generations rise and pass away, the strength of those who labour and suffer, and the repose of the holy and blessed dead: we rejoice in the communion of your saints.

We remember all who have faithfully lived and died, especially those most dear to us.

And to your name, O Lord, with the Church on earth and the Church in heaven, we ascribe all honour and glory, world without end.

Eternal God and Father,
   whose love is stronger than death:
we rejoice that the dead as well as the living
   are in your love and care;
and as we remember with thanksgiving
   those who have gone before us in the way of Christ,
we pray that we may be counted worthy
   to share with them the life of your kingdom;
through Jesus Christ our Lord.

A collect

O ALMIGHTY God, who hast knit together thine elect in one communion and fellowship, in the mystical body of thy Son Christ our Lord: grant us grace so to follow thy blessed saints in all virtuous and godly living, that we may come to those unspeakable joys, which thou hast prepared for them that unfeignedly love thee; through Jesus Christ our Lord.

THE HOPE OF HEAVEN

BRING us, O Lord God, at our last awakening into the house and gate of heaven, to enter into that gate and dwell in that house, where there shall be no darkness nor dazzling, but one equal light; no noise nor silence, but one equal music; no fears nor hopes, but one equal possession; no ends or beginnings, but one equal eternity; in the habitations of your glory and dominion, world without end.

We thank you, O Lord our God,
    that the life which we now live in Christ
is part of the life which is eternal,
    and the fellowship which we have with him
unites us with your whole Church
    on earth and in heaven:
and we pray that as we journey through the years
    we may know joys which are without end,
and at the last come to that abiding city
    where you reign for evermore.

JOURNEY'S END

FATHER, we pray for all who are finding the last stage of their journey a sore trial to flesh or spirit:
    the seriously ill,
    the elderly and infirm,
    and the dying.
Keep them in the fellowship of all faithful souls on earth and in heaven; and bring us all, through time and through death, to our fulfilment in life eternal, through our Lord Jesus Christ.

Grant, O Lord, that we may ever walk in your presence, with your love in our hearts, your truth in our minds, your strength in our wills, that when we finally stand before you, it may be with the assurance of your welcome and the joy of our homecoming.

We pray, gracious Father, for those whose earthly life is drawing to its end, that you will grant to them the comfort of your presence. Relieve all distress, remove every fear, and give peace now and at the last, through Jesus Christ our Lord.

May God in his infinite love and mercy bring the whole Church, living and departed in the Lord Jesus, to a joyful resurrection and the fulfilment of his eternal kingdom.

FOR THE DAY

LORD, on the way of goodness,
  when we stumble, hold us;
    when we fall, lift us up
    when we are hard pressed by evil, deliver us;
    when we turn from what is good, turn us back;
    and bring us at last to your glory.

O Lord, support us all the day long of this troublous life, until the shadows lengthen, and the evening comes, and the busy world is hushed, the fever of life is over, and our work is done. Then, Lord, in your mercy, grant us safe lodging, a holy rest, and peace at the last; through Jesus Christ our Lord.

HYMN

THE BLESSING

MONDAY

Children at school

O GOD our Father, we pray for the children growing up in our schools as they prepare for their tasks in life.

May they learn the lessons of greatest worth: self-discipline, integrity of character, care for others, and a true sense of values.

So may they acquire wisdom as well as knowledge, and be strong in spirit to serve their generation and to further your will; through Jesus Christ our Lord.

Housewives

Be present with us, O God, in our daily duties, and give your strength and protection to those whose work is in their home and family circle. Support them in all times of difficulty and anxiety, and make them to know that in ministering to the needs of others they are serving the Lord Christ.

The incurable

Heavenly Father, we pray for those who suffer from incurable diseases.

May they remember always that their infirmities are of the physical body which withers away, and come to discover that their condition can be a way through difficulty to a deeper awareness of the life of the spirit.

Through the pain and weariness of illness may they know that they are not alone, and in fellowship with Christ learn to understand better the sufferings of others.

Those who serve in Parliament

Almighty God, direct the hearts and minds of those who bear in their hands the government of this people.

Make them to uphold honour and justice, to restrain evil and oppression, and to seek the true prosperity of our nation and the welfare of all mankind; through Jesus Christ our Lord.

The homeless and badly housed

O God, whose will it is that none should live without comfort and hope, have compassion on the many in our land who have no home of their own, or live in over-crowded dwellings. Bless and inspire those who are labouring for their good. Stir the conscience of the whole nation; break the bonds of covetousness; and make plain the way of deliverance, for the sake of Jesus Christ our Saviour.

Race relations

Grant us, O Lord, to see in our fellow countrymen of whatever colour or race brothers and sisters for whom Christ died.

Give us grace to welcome people of different cultures and beliefs into our national life, and the humility to receive from them such good things as they have to offer.

Save us all from racial prejudice and indifference to the stranger; and grant that we may inherit the freedom of the sons and daughters of God in Christ Jesus, the Lord and Saviour of all.

The Church's witness today

We pray, O God, for the Church in the world of today:

that it may be true to its gospel and responsive to the needs of mankind;

that it may conserve what is good in the past and reach out boldly to the future;

that it may care for the individual and help to change society;

and that it may have a growing unity without sacrificing all variety of response to your grace.

We ask it in the name of Jesus Christ our Lord.

TUESDAY

Our homes

O JESUS Christ, our brother, our Lord: you lived in a home at Nazareth; you obeyed your parents, worked with your father, and enjoyed the company of your friends and relations. We ask you to bless our homes, to strengthen the love that we have one for another, and to give us all that we need for our welfare and happiness; for your name's sake.

Those who are ill

O God, the Creator and Father of all men, we praise you that your will is life and health and strength. Help all who are ill or in pain to place themselves in your hands in loving trust, so that your healing life may flow into them to make them well and strong, able and ready to do your will; through Jesus Christ our Lord.

The persecuted

To those who this day suffer persecution and oppression, give courage, O Lord Christ, and hope beyond themselves, and faith in God. Shorten their trial, bring them deliverance, and amid fear, suffering and grief may love and justice prevail.

The life of the nation

We pray, O God, for this our country; that as a people we may seek service before privilege, peace before self-preservation, and may share prosperity rather than seek private gain, setting the honour of your name before our own. We ask it through Jesus Christ our Lord.

The hungry and destitute

Almighty God, Father of all mankind, we bring before you the need and despair of those whose lives are impoverished by the hostility and strife of men.

Prosper the efforts of all who are working to provide homes for the destitute and food for the hungry.

Give understanding of these issues to the leaders of the nations, that they may be just and merciful in all their dealings; and unite us all in a common obedience to your will; through Jesus Christ our Lord.

The bereaved

Almighty God, whose Son our Lord Jesus Christ won the victory over death: grant that all who mourn the loss of those dear to them may enter into his victory, and find comfort, hope and peace in him, who is the resurrection and the life.

Animals

Lord God, who made the earth and every living creature: help us to treat with compassion the animals entrusted to our care, that they may not suffer from our neglect nor become the victims of any cruelty; and grant that in caring for them we may find a deeper understanding of your love for all creation; through Jesus Christ our Lord.

WEDNESDAY

Parents

OUR Father, we ask the grace of understanding love for fathers and mothers in the cares and responsibilities of family life; that in ministering to their children they may build up in their home a fellowship of service and compassion which will reflect the light of your presence to those around; for the sake of Jesus Christ our Lord.

The rising generation

Lord, for the vision of youth, its love of justice, strength of purpose and honesty of mind, we bring our thanks and praise. Make plain your living word to the rising generation, that they may grow up in the faith of Christ to love and honour your name and to render service to others.

Those engaged in industry

O God our Father, whose Son Jesus Christ worked in the carpenter's shop at Nazareth, we pray for all involved in our industrial life. Grant increase of understanding and co-operation between management and labour, that together they may seek what is just and wise, and work in harmony for the benefit of mankind.

Farmers

Almighty God, by whose blessing the earth brings forth abundantly all that is needful for the life of man: prosper the work of farmers and those engaged in agriculture; that with thankful hearts they may reap the fruit of their labour, and we and all mankind may rejoice in your great goodness; through Jesus Christ our Lord.

International co-operation

God and Father of all, who created mankind in your own image but with many differences of character and culture: we pray for those who represent their countries in the United Nations Organisation; that through their counsels each nation may reach its own maturity, and the whole world may realise a unity rich enough to express all the manifold variety of your creation; through Jesus Christ our Lord.

Those who influence others

We pray, O God, for those who as writers, speakers and entertainers influence the thought of our people through the press, radio and television.

Help them to exercise their gifts with responsibility and understanding, that they may enrich the common life of the nation and strengthen the forces of truth and goodness; through Jesus Christ our Lord.

The hidden Christ

Eternal Lord Christ, we praise you that since the beginning of history you have worked unrecognised as the wisdom and light of men.

We praise you that your name became known in a human life, in the humility of Bethlehem, the love of Calvary, and the glory of your resurrection.

Help us to see you still at work in everything that is holy, true, and good; and grant that we for our part may delight to work humbly and unrecognised, desiring only that your loving purpose shall go forward, until all come to see you as the hidden heart of all things.

THURSDAY

Our daily work

GOD our Father, we thank you for calling us through your Son Jesus Christ to be ministers of your love in the world: help us to obey this calling in the place where we work, in our homes and in our society, that we may be quick to seize occasions of service, and wise to use them with loving care, for the honour of our Lord.

Teachers

Lord Jesus Christ, you showed on earth your love for children and welcomed those who were brought to you: we ask you to guide with your Spirit those who are called to be teachers in the schools of this land; that nothing may hinder our children from growing in faith and in the knowledge of your love, and that your name may be honoured in the life of our nation.

Space travel

O Lord our God, the heavens declare your glory, and the moon and the stars which you have ordained; yet you have given man dominion over the works of your hands.

We pray for those who travel far beyond the bounds of earth; that the skill and knowledge of scientists, technicians and aeronauts may be used for the benefit of all men, and for your glory.

The peace of the world

Lord God, we pray that your holy and life-giving Spirit may so move in the hearts of men, and among the nations of the world, that the barriers of fear, suspicion and hatred which separate us may crumble, and the body of mankind, being healed of its divisions, may be united in the bonds of justice and peace; through Jesus Christ our Lord.

Children in need

God and Father of all, we commend to your compassion all homeless children and orphans, and all whose lives are overshadowed by violence, or thwarted by disease. Awaken in us all your living charity, and bless those who work for the welfare of children in any kind of need; through Jesus Christ our Lord.

Prisoners

We pray, our Father, for those whose freedom has been taken from them:

for all who suffer imprisonment, whether for crime or for conscience sake;

for all whose vision of your world is seen through bars, and in whose heart the lamp of hope burns low.

God of mercy, give them help according to their need, and hear our prayer for Jesus Christ's sake.

The Church's witness

God and Father of all, whose love recognises no barriers of nation, race or colour, we ask your blessing on the Church of Jesus Christ in all the world; that through the witness of its faith, its worship and its life, your way may be known upon earth, your saving power among all nations, for the glory of your name.

Leaders of the nation

WE pray, O God, for your servant Elizabeth our Queen, for the ministers of the Crown and all members of parliament. Guide those who rule over us and help them to govern in your faith and fear; and enable them so to order our national life that selfishness and injustice may be defeated, and all may strive together for the common good; to the praise and honour of your name.

Racial reconciliation

Father, who formed the family of man to live in harmony and peace: we acknowledge before you our divisions, quarrels, hatreds, injustices and greed.

May your Church demonstrate before the world the power of the gospel to destroy divisions, so that in Christ Jesus there may be no barriers of wealth or class, age or intellect, race or colour, but all may be equally your children, members one of another and heirs together of your everlasting kingdom.

Those in mental distress

Lord Jesus Christ, who for love of our souls entered the deep darkness of the cross:

we pray that your love may surround all who are in the darkness of great mental distress and who find it difficult to pray for themselves.

May they know that darkness and light are both alike to you and that you have promised never to fail them or forsake them.

The hallowing of marriage

O God our Father, from whom every family in heaven and on earth is named: we pray that marriage may be held in honour, that husbands and wives may live faithfully together, and that the members of every family may grow in mutual love and understanding, bearing one another's burdens and so fulfilling the law of Christ.

Judges and magistrates

Almighty God, Judge eternal and most merciful Saviour, give to the judges and magistrates of our land the humility, insight and compassion needful to those who pass judgment on their fellow men, and the courage always to uphold the cause of truth and justice; through Jesus Christ our Lord.

Seafarers

We pray, O God, for all seafarers as they fulfil the duties and face the dangers of their calling:

the officers and men of the Royal Navy and Merchant Navy;

the keepers of lighthouses, the crews of lightships and weather ships, the pilots of our ports;

all who carry out the services of docks and harbours;

and those who man lifeboats and guard our coasts.

Grant them your strength and protection, and keep them in the hour of special need; for Jesus Christ's sake.

The victims of war

Almighty God, Father of all men, we bring to you in prayer those of every nation who are suffering through war: the wounded and disabled, the homeless and bereaved, and all the starving and destitute multitudes of our world.

Give us a heart of compassion, O Lord, that by prayer and action we may help those who are working to relieve their need. We ask it in Christ's name.

SATURDAY

Those engaged in scientific research

ETERNAL God, Creator and Lord of all things, you have given men minds and wills to discover the secrets of the universe: give vision and courage to those engaged in scientific work, that by their patient studies and research we may advance in our understanding of your purpose for the world, and be better able to serve the needs and welfare of mankind.

Christian unity

Father, we pray for your Church throughout the world, that it may share to the full in the work of your Son, revealing you to men and reconciling men to you and to one another; that we and all Christian people may learn to love one another as you have loved us, and your Church may more and more reflect the unity which is your will and your gift in Jesus Christ our Lord.

Users of the roads

O God our Father, give to us and to all who use the roads watchfulness and care and consideration for others; that death and injury may be caused to none, and all who travel may complete their journey in safety and peace; through Jesus Christ our Lord.

Local government

We pray, O God, for those who hold office in local government, and for all who in various ways serve the community; that fulfilling their duties with singleness of purpose, they may wisely and faithfully exercise the authority committed to them and promote the common good; through Jesus Christ our Lord.

Music and musicians

Eternal Lord God, source of all beauty and harmony, we praise you for the gift of music:
for the inspiration given to those who compose it,
for the skill and devotion of those who perform it,
for the faculties and powers which enable us to enjoy it;
and we pray that as by this gift our lives are enriched and renewed, so we may glorify you in a fuller dedication of ourselves, giving thanks always for all things in the name of our Lord Jesus Christ.

Foreign policy

God and Father of all, you have taught us to care for one another and to live in peace: grant that our policies toward other nations may be dictated not by self-interest but by concern for the common good, and that we may seek to further the cause of justice and freedom in the world; through Jesus Christ our Lord.

People of other religions

Heavenly Father, help us as Christians to gain a deeper insight into the beliefs of those who practise other religions, so that we may better understand our differences and share our common convictions, and go forward in faith to learn more of your truth; through Jesus Christ our Lord.

BLESSINGS AND ASCRIPTIONS

THE grace of our Lord Jesus Christ, and the love of God, and the fellowship of the Holy Spirit, be with us all evermore.

Grace to you and peace from God the Father, and our Lord Jesus Christ.

The God of hope fill you with all joy and peace in believing, so that by the power of the Holy Spirit you may abound in hope.

The grace of our Lord Jesus Christ be with you all.

May the God of peace, who brought again from the dead our Lord Jesus, the great shepherd of the sheep, equip you with everything good, that you may do his will, working in you that which is pleasing in his sight, through Jesus Christ, to whom be glory for ever and ever.

The God of all grace, who has called you to his eternal glory in Christ, restore, establish, and strengthen you. To him be the dominion for ever and ever.

Now to him who by the power at work within us is able to do far more abundantly than all that we ask or think, to him be glory in the Church and in Christ Jesus to all generations, for ever and ever.

Now to him who is able to keep you from falling, and to present you without blemish before the presence of his glory with rejoicing, to the only God our Saviour, be glory and majesty, might and authority, through Jesus Christ our Lord, before all time, now, and for evermore.

To the King of ages, immortal, invisible, the only God, be honour and glory for ever and ever.

The God of peace himself sanctify you wholly; and may your spirit and soul and body be preserved entire, without blame at the coming of our Lord Jesus Christ.

Blessing and glory and wisdom and thanksgiving and honour and power and might be to our God for ever and ever.

The peace of God, which passes all understanding, keep your hearts and minds in the knowledge and love of God, and of his Son Jesus Christ our Lord; and the blessing of God almighty, the Father, the Son, and the Holy Spirit, be among you, and remain with you always.

To God's gracious mercy and protection we commit you.
The Lord bless you and keep you.
The Lord make his face to shine upon you and be gracious to you.
The Lord lift up his countenance upon you, and give you peace.

May the blessing of God almighty, the Father, the Son, and the Holy Spirit, rest upon you; may he give light to guide you, courage to support you, and love to unite you, now and evermore.

May the love of the Lord Jesus draw you to himself;
may the power of the Lord Jesus strengthen you in his service;
may the joy of the Lord Jesus fill your souls;
and the blessing of God almighty, the Father, the Son, and the Holy Spirit, be upon you and remain with you for ever.

Go forth into the world in peace; be of good courage; hold fast that which is good; render to no man evil for evil; strengthen the faint-hearted; support the weak; help the afflicted; honour all men; love and serve the Lord, rejoicing in the power of the Holy Spirit. And the blessing of God almighty, the Father, the Son, and the Holy Spirit, be upon you, and remain with you for ever.

Blessing and honour and thanksgiving and praise,
    more than we can utter,
    more than we can conceive,
be yours, O holy and glorious Trinity,
    Father, Son, and Holy Spirit,
by all angels, all men, all creatures,
    for ever and ever.

To God the Father, who loved us, and made us accepted in the Beloved;

to God the Son, who loved us, and washed us from our sins by his own blood;

to God the Holy Spirit, who sheds the love of God abroad in our hearts:

to the one true God be all love and all glory, for time and for eternity.

The almighty and merciful Lord, the Father, the Son, and the Holy Spirit, bless and preserve us.

May grace, mercy, and peace, from God the Father, Son, and Holy Spirit, be with you all, this day and for evermore.

May the Lord bless you, and preserve you from all evil, and bring you to everlasting life.

May the blessing of God almighty, the Father, the Son, and the Holy Spirit, rest upon you and upon your homes, this day and evermore.

May the blessing of the Lord rest upon you and upon all his people, in every land, of every tongue, now and evermore.

1. NEW YEAR

GIVE us grace, O God, to begin this year in your faith, and to continue it in your favour; that being guided in all our doings, and guarded all our days, we may spend our lives in your service and glorify your holy name; through Jesus Christ our Lord.

Heavenly Father, whose mercy is everlasting: accept our thanksgiving for all the blessings of the year that is past. Take our lives afresh into your keeping as we face the unknown future, and fit us by your grace for whatever lies before us in the days to come; for the sake of Jesus Christ our Lord.

2. PASSIONTIDE

ALMIGHTY God, whose beloved Son, for our sake, willingly offered himself to endure the cross, its agony and its shame: remove from us all coldness and cowardice of heart, and give us grace to take up our cross and follow him, even the same our Lord and Saviour Jesus Christ.

O God, who by the passion of your Son our Saviour Jesus Christ showed us the greatness of true humility and the meaning of sacrificial love: give us grace to serve one another in all lowliness of spirit, and to enter into the fellowship of his sufferings; who is now alive and reigns with you and the Holy Spirit, one God, for ever and ever.

Lord Jesus Christ, betrayed for thirty pieces of silver, deserted by your disciples, denied by Peter, mocked by Herod, scourged by Pilate, crowned with thorns, and nailed to the cross: humbly and with all our heart we thank you for your suffering and death, by which we have been forgiven and redeemed.

O God, we are not worthy of this your greatest gift, that Christ shed his blood for us. Forgive us that we are so slow to respond and to show the gratitude we owe in faithful service and loving deed; and help us, as we hear the story of the cross once again this passiontide, to become alive to what it meant to him, and what it involves for us.

O God, fill us with the divine humility of Christ; that having the same mind that was also in him, we may look not every one on his own things, but every one also on the things of others, emptying our wills of pride and our hearts of complaining, and laying down our glories before the cross.

Lord Jesus Christ, who in the week of your passion cleansed the temple in Jerusalem: purify our hearts from all defilement, our worship from all insincerity, and our lives from all selfishness; that we may become a holy temple in the Lord, a dwelling place of God in the Spirit.

O Lord and Saviour, who on the night before your passion took towel and water and washed the feet of your disciples: give us understanding of what you have done, and teach us to follow the example of your humility, that by love we may serve one another for your sake.

3. THE QUEEN'S BIRTHDAY AND COMMONWEALTH DAY

Pour your blessing, O God, upon Elizabeth our Queen, that she may fulfil her calling as a Christian ruler. Support her in the ceaseless round of duty, inspire her in the service of many people. Give her wise and loyal ministers; bless her in home and family; and grant that through her the Commonwealth may be knit together in one great brotherhood, a joy and strength to all its members and an instrument of your wise and loving will; through Jesus Christ our Lord.

From the Accession Service

Almighty God, who rulest over all the kingdoms of the world, and dost order them according to thy good pleasure: we give thee hearty thanks for that thou hast set thy servant our sovereign lady, Queen Elizabeth, upon the throne of this realm. Let thy wisdom be her guide, and thine arm strengthen her; let truth and justice, holiness and righteousness, peace and charity, abound in her days; and direct all her counsels and endeavours to thy glory, and the welfare of her subjects; through Jesus Christ our Lord.

4. UNITED NATIONS' DAY

GOD and Father of all mankind, we ask your blessing on the United Nations' Organisation, that through it righteousness may be established in international relationships, fear and suspicion may be removed and a lasting peace ensured; through him who has shown to man the ways of justice, mercy and reconciliation, your Son our Saviour Jesus Christ.

5. CHRISTMAS

GRANT us, O God, such love and wonder that with humble shepherds, wise men, and pilgrims unknown, we may come and adore the holy Babe, the heavenly King, and with our gifts worship and serve him, our Lord and Saviour Jesus Christ.

O God our Father, who by the birth of your Son Jesus Christ enlightened the darkness of the world: we pray that the light of your presence may shine more and more into the lives of men; that being filled with the spirit of good-will, the nations may inherit that gift of peace which he came to bring.

O Lord our God, who manifested your love to us by sending your only Son into the world, that we might live through him: grant us by your Holy Spirit the precious gift of faith, by which we may know that the Son of God has come; and help us to join our praises with the song of the heavenly host: Glory to God in the highest, and on earth peace, goodwill towards men.

Heavenly Father, we pray that amid all the joys and festivities of this season we may not forget what Christmas really means: that you loved the world so much that you gave your only Son, who was born to be our Saviour. Accept our thanksgiving, and fill us with the spirit of charity and goodwill, that we may show our gratitude in generous service to those who need our help; for Jesus Christ's sake.

Son of Man, our friend and brother, you were born in a stable, because there was no room in the inn. While we celebrate your birthday in the comfort of our homes this Christmas time we remember those who have no home, and all who live in sordid dwellings. Give us understanding of their need; show us what we can do to help; and make us generous in our love and gifts, because of Bethlehem, because of your love for us all.

A collect

God, who makest us glad with the yearly remembrance of the birth of thy only Son Jesus Christ: grant that as we joyfully receive him for our Redeemer, so we may with sure confidence behold him when he shall come to be our Judge; who liveth and reigneth with thee and the Holy Spirit, one God, world without end.

6. AT EVENING

O GOD, with whom there is no darkness, but the night shines as the day: keep and defend us and all your children through the coming night. Renew our hearts with your forgiveness, and our bodies with untroubled sleep, that we may wake to use more faithfully your gift of life; through Jesus Christ our Lord.

Two ancient prayers

Be present, O merciful God, and protect us through the hours of this night; so that we who are wearied by the changes and chances of this fleeting world may repose upon thy eternal changelessness; through Jesus Christ our Lord.

Watch thou, dear Lord, with those who wake, or watch, or weep tonight, and give thine angels charge over those who sleep. Tend thy sick ones, O Lord Christ. Rest thy weary ones. Bless thy dying ones. Soothe thy suffering ones. Pity thine afflicted ones. And all for thy love's sake.

7. BEFORE AN ELECTION

D IRECT, O Lord our God, the minds of those who are called upon to elect fit persons to serve in the parliament of our nation, that they may exercise their responsibility in such a way as to promote your glory and the welfare of this people; and to those who shall be elected give understanding hearts, sound judgment, and a concern for the common good; through Jesus Christ our Lord.

Look in mercy, O God, upon the citizens of this country at the present time, that men and women of ability and integrity, wise, compassionate and upright, may be chosen to represent us in the high court of parliament; to the end that our nation may be led in the ways of righteousness, freedom and peace, to the honour of your name.

8. IN TIME OF NATIONAL EMERGENCY

GRANT, O Lord our God, that in this time of testing our people may know your presence and seek to obey your righteous will; that with integrity and courage we may accomplish the tasks you give us to do, and endure all that we are called upon to bear; through Jesus Christ our Lord.

God and Father of all, look upon us with your mercy, and in this time of strife and unrest give to us as a nation a fuller realisation of our brotherhood, man with man. Allay all anger and bitterness, and deepen in us a sense of truth and equity in our dealings one with another; for the sake of Jesus Christ our Lord.

9. IN TIME OF NATIONAL MOURNING

LOOK graciously upon us, O Lord our God, in this time of our nation's sorrow and loss. Give us comfort, keep us steadfast, uphold our faith, and enable us to find in you our refuge and our strength, now and always.

10. IN TIME OF WAR

For the armed forces

O GOD, our refuge and strength, a very present help in trouble, we commend to your mercy and protection the men and women who through perils of war are serving

this nation. Take into your hands both them and the cause
they serve. Be with them in the midst of danger; and make
them bold, through death or life, to put their trust in you;
through Jesus Christ our Lord.

For the suffering

God of all grace, have in your keeping the many who at
this time are suffering through war: the wounded, the
sick, and the prisoners; the homeless and the oppressed;
the anxious and the bereaved. Uphold them, O Lord, in
their hour of need, and raise up friends to help them, for
the sake of him who bore for us the agony of the cross,
our Saviour Jesus Christ.

For prisoners

Merciful Father, look with your tender compassion on
all prisoners of war. Let your love protect and cheer them;
give them courage to endure patiently in the midst of
weariness and hardship; and hasten the time of their release;
through Jesus Christ our Lord.

For peace

Almighty God, in whose power it is to bring good out
of evil and cause even the wrath of man to turn to your
praise: in your great mercy so order and dispose the issue
of this war that we may be brought through strife to a just
and lasting peace, and the nations of the world may be
united in a stronger fellowship for the promotion of your
glory and the good of all mankind.

THE EPIPHANY OF OUR LORD

Arise, shine, for thy light has come, and the glory of the Lord has risen upon thee.

ALMIGHTY God, who made known the incarnation of your Son by the bright shining of a star, which when the wise men saw they adored your majesty and presented gifts: we pray that the star of your righteousness may always shine in our hearts, and that for our treasure we may offer you our love and service, our worship and thanksgiving.

HYMN

ALMIGHTY and everlasting God, who by the guidance of a star led the magi from eastern lands to adore the newborn King:

we praise you for giving your Son Jesus Christ to be the light of the world, and for revealing in him your saving love to all mankind.

We praise you for the light of the everlasting gospel sent forth to every nation, kindred and people, and shining so long among us.

We praise you for your Church universal, the whole company of Christ's people, worshipping him and bearing witness to him throughout the earth.

Accept, O Lord, the praise we bring, and fill the world with the light of your glory, that all men may come and render homage to Christ their Saviour and their King.

OUR FATHER...

THE ASCENSION DAY

Lift up your heads, O ye gates, and be ye lift up, ye ever-
lasting doors, and the King of glory shall come in.

ALMIGHTY God, whose Son our Saviour Jesus Christ
ascended far above all heavens that he might fill all
things: grant us to know that according to his promise he
abides always with his Church on earth, even to the end
of the world; through the same Jesus Christ our Lord.

HYMN

LORD God almighty, we praise you that you have exalted
your Son Jesus Christ to your right hand and have
crowned him with glory and honour, because he suffered
death for us all.

We rejoice in him, our great High Priest, who has
entered once for all into the holy place, and ever lives to
intercede on our behalf.

Grant that we, sanctified by the offering of his body,
may draw near with a true heart in full assurance of faith
by the new and living way he has dedicated for us, and
present our bodies a living sacrifice.

Through the same our Lord Jesus Christ, who is alive
and reigns with you, O Father, and the Holy Spirit, one
God, world without end.

OUR FATHER...

THE CIRCUMCISION OF CHRIST (January 1)

ALMIGHTY God, who madest thy blessed Son to be circumcised, and obedient to the law for man: grant us the true circumcision of the Spirit; that, our hearts, and all our members, being mortified from all worldly and carnal lusts, we may in all things obey thy blessed will; through the same thy Son Jesus Christ our Lord.

The Naming of Jesus

Heavenly Father, who in the naming of thine incarnate Son Jesus didst declare thy purpose of salvation to all mankind: grant that every tongue may confess that Jesus Christ is Lord, to thy eternal glory; through the same Jesus Christ our Lord.

THE EPIPHANY (January 6)

O GOD, who by the leading of a star didst manifest thy only-begotten Son to the Gentiles: mercifully grant that we, who know thee now by faith, may after this life have the fruition of thy glorious Godhead; through Jesus Christ our Lord.

THE CONVERSION OF ST PAUL (January 25)

O GOD, who through the preaching of the blessed apostle Saint Paul, hast caused the light of the gospel to shine throughout the world: grant, we beseech thee, that we, having his wonderful conversion in remembrance, may show forth our thankfulness unto thee for the same, by following the holy doctrine which he taught; through Jesus Christ our Lord.

THE PRESENTATION OF CHRIST IN THE TEMPLE
(February 2)

ALMIGHTY and everlasting God, we humbly beseech thy Majesty, that, as thy only-begotten Son was this day presented in the temple in substance of our flesh, so we may be presented unto thee with pure and clean hearts, by the same thy Son Jesus Christ our Lord.

ASH WEDNESDAY

ALMIGHTY and everlasting God, who hatest nothing that thou hast made, and dost forgive the sins of all them that are penitent: create and make in us new and contrite hearts, that we worthily lamenting our sins, and acknowledging our wretchedness, may obtain of thee, the God of all mercy, perfect remission and forgiveness; through Jesus Christ our Lord.

ST MATTHIAS (February 24)

O ALMIGHTY God, who into the place of the traitor Judas didst choose thy faithful servant Matthias to be of the number of the twelve apostles: grant that thy Church, being always preserved from false apostles, may be ordered and guided by faithful and true pastors; through Jesus Christ our Lord.

ST DAVID (March 1)

O GOD, who madest Saint David to be a victorious champion of the faith, and didst reward his rich sowing with an abundant harvest: continue thy favour, we beseech thee, towards the people of Wales and the Church in their midst; and so bless them with spiritual gifts that the land of their fathers may be a praise in all the earth; through Jesus Christ our Lord.

ST PATRICK (March 17)

ALMIGHTY God, who by thy providence didst choose thy servant Saint Patrick to be the apostle of the Irish people, that the light of the gospel might shine in their midst: grant that they may so walk in that light that they may show forth thy glory before the world, and come at last to thy eternal kingdom; through Jesus Christ our Lord.

THE ANNUNCIATION OF THE BLESSED VIRGIN MARY (March 25)

WE beseech thee, O Lord, pour thy grace into our hearts; that, as we have known the incarnation of thy Son Jesus Christ by the message of an angel, so by his cross and passion we may be brought unto the glory of his resurrection; through the same Jesus Christ our Lord.

GOOD FRIDAY

ALMIGHTY God, we beseech thee graciously to behold this thy family, for which our Lord Jesus Christ was contented to be betrayed, and given up into the hands of wicked men, and to suffer death upon the cross, who now liveth and reigneth with thee and the Holy Spirit, ever one God, world without end.

EASTER EVE

GRANT, O Lord, that as we are baptised into the death of thy blessed Son our Saviour Jesus Christ, so by continual mortifying our corrupt affections we may be buried with him; and that, through the grave, and gate of death, we may pass to our joyful resurrection; for his merits, who died, and was buried, and rose again for us, thy Son Jesus Christ our Lord.

ST GEORGE (April 23)

O LORD God of hosts, who didst give grace unto Saint George to lay aside the fear of man, and to confess thee even unto death: grant that the people of England may steadfastly cleave to the same faith, and yield true allegiance to the Captain of our salvation; to whom, with thee and the Holy Spirit, be praise from all the armies of thy saints, now and evermore.

ST MARK (April 25)

O ALMIGHTY God, who hast instructed thy holy Church with the heavenly doctrine of thy evangelist Saint Mark: give us grace, that, being not like children carried away with every blast of vain doctrine, we may be established in the truth of thy holy gospel; through Jesus Christ our Lord.

ST PHILIP AND ST JAMES (May 1)

O ALMIGHTY God, whom truly to know is everlasting life: grant us perfectly to know thy Son Jesus Christ to be the way, the truth, and the life; that, following the steps of thy holy apostles, Saint Philip and Saint James, we may steadfastly walk in the way that leadeth to eternal life; through the same thy Son Jesus Christ our Lord.

THE ASCENSION DAY

GRANT, we beseech thee, Almighty God, that like as we do believe thy only-begotten Son our Lord Jesus Christ to have ascended into the heavens; so we may also in heart and mind thither ascend, and with him continually dwell, who liveth and reigneth with thee and the Holy Spirit, one God, world without end.

ST BARNABAS (June 11)

O LORD God Almighty, who didst endue thy holy apostle Barnabas with singular gifts of the Holy Spirit: leave us not, we beseech thee, destitute of thy manifold gifts, nor yet of grace to use them always to thy honour and glory; through Jesus Christ our Lord.

ST JOHN BAPTIST (June 24)

ALMIGHTY God, by whose providence thy servant John Baptist was wonderfully born, and sent to prepare the way of thy Son our Saviour, by preaching of repentance: make us so to follow his doctrine and holy life, that we may truly repent according to his preaching; and after his example constantly speak the truth, boldly rebuke vice, and patiently suffer for the truth's sake; through Jesus Christ our Lord.

ST PETER (June 29)

O ALMIGHTY God, who by thy Son Jesus Christ didst give to thy apostle Saint Peter many excellent gifts, and commandedst him earnestly to feed thy flock: make, we beseech thee, all bishops and pastors diligently to preach thy holy word, and the people obediently to follow the same, that they may receive the crown of everlasting glory; through Jesus Christ our Lord.

ST MARY MAGDALEN (July 22)

O ALMIGHTY God, whose blessed Son did call and sanctify Mary Magdalen to be a witness to his resurrection: mercifully grant that by thy grace we may be healed of all our infirmities, and always serve thee in the power of his endless life, who with thee and the Holy Spirit liveth and reigneth, one God, world without end.

ṢT JAMES (July 25)

GRANT, O merciful God, that as thine holy apostle Saint James, leaving his father and all that he had, without delay was obedient unto the calling of thy Son Jesus Christ, and followed him; so we, forsaking all worldly and carnal affections, may be evermore ready to follow thy holy commandments; through Jesus Christ our Lord.

THE TRANSFIGURATION (August 6)

O GOD, who before the passion of thine only-begotten Son didst reveal his glory upon the holy mount: grant unto us thy servants, that in faith beholding the light of his countenance, we may be strengthened to bear the cross, and be changed into his likeness from glory to glory; through the same Jesus Christ our Lord.

ST BARTHOLOMEW (August 24)

O ALMIGHTY and everlasting God, who didst give to thine apostle Bartholomew grace truly to believe and to preach thy word: grant, we beseech thee, unto thy Church, to love that word which he believed, and both to preach and receive the same; through Jesus Christ our Lord.

ST MATTHEW (September 21)

O ALMIGHTY God, who by thy blessed Son didst call Matthew from the receipt of custom to be an apostle and evangelist: grant us grace to forsake all covetous desires, and inordinate love of riches, and to follow the same thy Son Jesus Christ, who liveth and reigneth with thee and the Holy Spirit, one God, world without end.

ST MICHAEL AND ALL ANGELS (September 29)

O EVERLASTING God, who hast ordained and constituted the services of angels and men in a wonderful order: mercifully grant, that as thy holy angels always do thee service in heaven, so by thy appointment they may succour and defend us on earth; through Jesus Christ our Lord.

ST LUKE (October 18)

A LMIGHTY God, who calledst Luke the physician, whose praise is in the gospel, to be an evangelist, and physician of the soul: may it please thee, that by the wholesome medicines of the doctrine delivered by him, all the diseases of our souls may be healed; through the merits of thy Son Jesus Christ our Lord.

ST SIMON AND ST JUDE (October 28)

O ALMIGHTY God, who hast built thy Church upon the foundation of the apostles and prophets, Jesus Christ himself being the head corner-stone: grant us so to be joined together in unity of spirit by their doctrine, that we may be made an holy temple acceptable unto thee; through Jesus Christ our Lord.

ALL SAINTS (November 1)

O ALMIGHTY God, who hast knit together thine elect in one communion and fellowship, in the mystical body of thy Son Jesus Christ our Lord: grant us grace so to follow thy blessed saints in all virtuous and godly living, that we may come to those unspeakable joys, which thou hast prepared for them that unfeignedly love thee; through Jesus Christ our Lord.

COMMEMORATION OF ALL SOULS (November 2)

O LORD, the maker and redeemer of all believers: grant to the faithful departed all the unsearchable benefits of thy Son's passion; that in the day of his appearing they may be manifested as thy true children; through the same thy Son Jesus Christ our Lord.

ST ANDREW (November 30)

ALMIGHTY God, who didst give such grace unto thy holy apostle Saint Andrew, that he readily obeyed the calling of thy Son Jesus Christ, and followed him without delay: grant unto us all, that we, being called by thy holy word, may forthwith give up ourselves to fulfil thy holy commandments; through the same Jesus Christ our Lord.

ST THOMAS (December 21)

ALMIGHTY and everlasting God, who for the more confirmation of the faith didst suffer thy holy apostle Thomas to be doubtful in thy Son's resurrection: grant us so perfectly, and without all doubt, to believe in thy Son Jesus Christ, that our faith in thy sight may never be reproved. Hear us, O Lord, through the same Jesus Christ, to whom, with thee and the Holy Spirit, be all honour and glory, now and for evermore.

CHRISTMAS DAY (December 25)

ALMIGHTY God, who hast given us thy only-begotten Son to take our nature upon him, and as at this time to be born of a pure Virgin: grant that we being regenerate, and made thy children by adoption and grace, may daily be renewed by thy Holy Spirit; through the same our Lord Jesus Christ, who liveth and reigneth with thee and the same Spirit, ever one God, world without end.

ST STEPHEN (December 26)

GRANT, O Lord, that in all our sufferings here upon earth for the testimony of thy truth, we may steadfastly look up to heaven, and by faith behold the glory that shall be revealed; and, being filled with the Holy Spirit, may learn to love and bless our persecutors by the example of thy first martyr Saint Stephen, who prayed for his murderers to thee, O blessed Jesus, who standest at the right hand of God to succour all those that suffer for thee, our only Mediator and Advocate.

ST JOHN THE EVANGELIST (December 27)

MERCIFUL Lord, we beseech thee to cast thy bright beams of light upon thy Church, that it being enlightened by the doctrine of thy blessed apostle and evangelist Saint John may so walk in the light of thy truth, that it may at length attain to the light of everlasting life; through Jesus Christ our Lord.

THE INNOCENTS (December 28)

O ALMIGHTY God, who out of the mouths of babes and sucklings hast ordained strength, and madest infants to glorify thee by their deaths: mortify and kill all vices in us, and so strengthen us by thy grace, that by the innocency of our lives, and constancy of our faith even unto death, we may glorify thy holy name; through Jesus Christ our Lord.

INDEX